Teachers' Writing Groups: Collaborative Inquiry and Reflection for Professional Growth

Teachers' Writing Groups: Collaborative Inquiry and Reflection for Professional Growth

Edited by

Sarah Robbins
George Seaman
Kathleen Blake Yancey
Dede Yow

Copyright © 2006 Kennesaw State University Press

All rights reserved. No part of this book may be used or reproduced in any manner without prior written consent of the publisher.

Kennesaw State University Press
Kennesaw State University
Building 27, Suite 220, Mailbox 2701
1000 Chastain Road
Kennesaw, GA 30144

Daniel S. Papp, President of the University
Lendley C. Black, Provost & Vice President for Academic Affairs
Laura S. Dabundo, Director of the Press
Shirley Parker-Cordell, Senior Administrative Specialist
Sarah L. Johnson, Promotion and Marketing Manager

Lindsie Jordan Tucker, Editor
Michelle R. Hinson, Production Editor & Book Design
Holly Miller, Cover Design
Cathleen Salsburg, Research Assistant

Library of Congress Cataloging-in-Publication Data

Teachers' writing groups : collaborative inquiry and reflection for professional growth / edited by Sarah Robbins ... [et al.].
    p. cm.
  ISBN-13: 978-1-933483-10-8
 1. Teachers--In-service training. 2. Teachers' workshops. 3. Authorship. I. Robbins, Sarah.
  LB1743.T43 2006
  370.71'5--dc22
                            2006032211

Printed in the United States of America

10 9 8 7 6 5 4 3 2 1

Contents

| Acknowledgments | ix |

Introduction

| ✓ ↜ Revisiting a Community of Practice in Action
Kathleen Blake Yancey, Sarah Robbins,
Dede Yow, and George Seaman | 1 |

Part I—Writing Group One: Creating Our Professional Identities

✓ ↜ The Gift of Time Deborah Kramb, Carol Harrell, George Seaman, and Dede Yow	17
↜ The Balancing Act: A Play on Managing Our Lives Deborah Kramb	23
↜ Writing Monster/Writing Mentor: Reading and Learning from Students' Stories of Writing Carol P. Harrell	39
↜ Build It and They Will Learn: Portfolios Revisited George Seaman	49
↜ Making Mentoring Visible Dede Yow	61

Part II—Writing Group Two: Looking Closely at Classroom Practices

↜ Reading to Write; "Reading" the Classroom to Re-vise Learning Sarah Robbins, Linda Stewart, and Renee Kaplan	75
↜ Sharing Journal Reflections of Inspiration and Remembrance in Holocaust Studies Renee Kaplan	81
↜ "Seeing" Community: Visual Culture in College Composition Sarah Robbins and Linda Stewart	97

Part III—Writing Group Three: Designing Writing Programs

- Social Revision — 115
  Victoria Walker, Leslie Walker, and Andy Smith
- Picture This: Using Wordless Books to Teach Primary-Grade Writers — 119
  Victoria Walker
- Re-envisioning the Writing Classroom — 135
  Leslie Walker
- Writing Groups Revised: Coaches, Community, and Craft in a Summer Institute — 149
  Andy Smith

Part IV—Re-viewing Writing Groups at Work

- Reading Across Writing Groups — 167
  Linda Stewart, Renee Kaplan, and Deborah Kramb
- Writing With Our Eyes Open: A Collaborative Response to *Teachers' Writing Groups* — 173
  Zsa Boykin, Toby Emert, Sandra Grant, and Scott Smoot
- Setting Teachers' Writing Groups in Context — 181
  Sarah Robbins, George Seaman, Dede Yow, and Kathleen Blake Yancey

Author Profiles — 198

Preface

This book was written by and for teachers interested in using writing and related collaborative learning processes to better understand classroom practice.

Many educators encourage their students to use writing as a tool for learning. However, writing is not as likely to be touted as a professional development strategy for teachers themselves. Recently, experts in staff development have been promoting teachers' study groups that use reading for shared learning. We are longtime fans of such work. But we also believe that professional growth can be enhanced substantially when teachers write, reflect, and revise as well as read together. This book comes out of a project based on that belief.

In a multi-year initiative, our project team formed several writing groups for teachers, and each group created its own protocols for managing its collaborative work. As our groups met to revise and reflect on our emerging narratives, we helped each other consider more deeply the theories that were driving the instructional practices we were writing about. In polishing our writing, we honed our thinking. In collaboratively shaping ideas about our teaching experiences, we improved our writing. Through this interactive process, we also enhanced our sense of ourselves as professionals.

Numerous times throughout the project, all three writing groups gathered to share stories of our processes, ask questions about our progress, and refine our ideas about writing to learn. A major strategy we used to promote this ongoing analysis was to generate individual and small-group reflections in response to structured prompts. Meanwhile, by thinking critically about the approaches we were developing for managing our writing groups, we identified strategies other educators can adapt to support collaborative learning.

Besides drawing on our book as a framework to support professional development, readers will also find vivid, engaging stories of individual teachers reflecting deeply on their own practices. Through writing these stories, all of us have strengthened our professional identities, in the classroom and beyond. Although ranging from primary through university-level educators, we came to see ourselves as a unified community of practice, meeting regularly and using shared reflection to grow together. In addition, we began to recognize how our particular community of practice was connected to other professionals engaged in related inquiry about teaching.

As you read this book now, we hope you will find helpful ways to use writing for professional development. And we also hope you will find colleagues with whom you can identify—educators like you, dedicated to teaching, committed to continued professionalization, and eager to share stories about our work.

Acknowledgments

The authors sharing their learning experiences in this book benefited enormously from working together. Along the way, a number of others made important contributions to our collaboration.

We thank the National Writing Project (NWP) for providing a mini-grant to our NWP site in the initial phase of our inquiry. That seed grant provided several release days for teachers to attend meetings, funds for the purchase of reading materials, and small stipends for our project participants.

Kennesaw State University also gave substantial support to our work, including a place to gather for writing group and whole-team meetings, access to computer labs for social writing opportunities, and permission to use such essentials as photocopying machines. In particular, we thank the English Department and the College of Humanities and Social Sciences, as well as the Bagwell College of Education, for hosting our project on numerous occasions.

Members of the community of local Kennesaw Mountain Writing Project (KMWP) NWP affiliates provided important encouragement for our research and writing. At a number of workshops and presentations sponsored by the KMWP, where we had the chance to share our work in progress, teacher colleagues asked probing questions and made insightful suggestions.

Special thanks go to the Kennesaw Mountain Writing Project's program staff, including Joe Cawley, Stacie Janecki, Amy Hopper, and Becky Ramsay.

Most of all, we are grateful to the many students whose classroom work is chronicled here. Their eagerness to contribute to our exploration helped each of us maintain faith that we would all grow together in ways beneficial to classroom teaching.

Acknowledgments

The authors sharing their learning experiences in this book benefited enormously from working together. Along the way, a number of others made important contributions to our collaboration.

We thank the National Writing Project (NWP) for providing a mini-grant to our NWP site in the initial phase of our inquiry. That seed grant provided several release days for teachers to attend meetings, funds for the purchase of reading materials, and small stipends for our project participants.

Kennesaw State University also gave substantial support to our work, including a place to gather for writing group and whole-team meetings, access to computer labs for social writing opportunities, and permission to use such essentials as photocopying machines. In particular, we thank the English Department and the College of Humanities and Social Sciences, as well as the Bagwell College of Education, for hosting our project on numerous occasions.

Members of the community of local Kennesaw Mountain Writing Project (KMWP) NWP affiliates provided important encouragement for our research and writing. At a number of workshops and presentations sponsored by the KMWP, where we had the chance to share our work in progress, teacher colleagues asked probing questions and made insightful suggestions.

Special thanks go to the Kennesaw Mountain Writing Project's program staff, including Joe Cawley, Stacie Janecki, Amy Hopper, and Becky Ramsay.

Most of all, we are grateful to the many students whose classroom work is chronicled here. Their eagerness to contribute to our exploration helped each of us maintain faith that we would all grow together in ways beneficial to classroom teaching.

Introduction: Revisiting a Community of Practice in Action

Kathleen Blake Yancey, Sarah Robbins, Dede Yow, and George Seaman

This book tells the story of how educators from a range of instructional settings—elementary school, middle school, high school, and college—formed an intentional community of practice focused on enhancing teaching and learning. Meeting, writing, and reflecting together, participants used sustained, shared inquiry to study their individual questions about teaching, while at the same time they also examined the specific learning practices being employed by several small writing groups and the larger team. On one level, then, our story demonstrates the potential that teachers' writing groups have to provide a mechanism for individuals' professional growth, a growth that includes the ability to make knowledge about teaching. On a second level, we also document in this volume how affiliating with a larger community of practice emphasizing collaborative reflection supported the groups' work. The goal behind telling this story is two-fold: (1) to provide specific examples of teacher knowledge created and refined in a "safe" collaborative inquiry space, itself composed through layered communities of practice hosting this project's work; and (2) to make visible the ways in which writing groups can facilitate teacher professionalization through reflective engagement and writing.

Our work together builds upon others' examination of social processes educators use for knowledge making, such as studies of how teachers use informal anecdotes (sometimes called "classroom lore") to generate shared understanding of their practices.[1] But our work has extended such earlier research by emphasizing, providing opportunities for, and studying processes of shared, structured reflection as avenues to teacher knowledge and professionalization. Perhaps most important, and notably different from projects on teacher study groups that have focused only on professional reading, writing was the central component of our learning. Though meeting independently for many sessions, our writing groups clearly benefited from being connected to the larger inquiry community assembled for this project. Indeed, our experience has shown that teachers who form small writing groups can profit from linking their work to larger support systems, such as school-improvement organizations or professional organizations like a National Writing Project site. By positioning their small-group learning within a support network, our project participants could study their own teaching in relational terms, building on scholarship and teaching practices beyond that most immediately available in their writing group. Interactions between the small writing groups and the larger project community promoted the development of a shared vocabulary as well, one whose major recurring terms we list below, with explanations to guide our readers now:

- inquiry: the process of studying open-ended questions, in this case through collaborative work of individuals and writing groups linked to our project;
- inquiry community: the entire group of teachers affiliated with the project, including the members of all the original writing groups and one group of readers who provided feedback to an early draft of the manuscript;
- protocols: regularized rules of behavior tried out and then self-consciously adapted within the writing groups, with different groups developing different protocols; parallel practices developed in the larger inquiry community;
- reflection: individual or group analysis based on retrospective thinking about a learning experience in action (see Schön below); may be carried out privately but more likely to be expressed orally or in writing within a collaborative context;
- professionalization: developing an enhanced identity as a teacher, based on acquisition of new knowledge and skills and the ability to share those with others;
- community of practice: a professionalized learning group using social strategies for acculturation and knowledge building, as in the research we outline below.

Our inquiry project situated itself from the outset within a broad tradition of scholarship on reflective practice as central to professional development and also within an emerging body of research on the special value that organized communities of practice can bring to such efforts. Crucial to this tradition has been the work of Donald Schön, whose influential books cut across a range of professional settings. When Schön began to publish on reflective practice, as in *The Reflective Practitioner* (1983), he did not focus on classroom teachers, but rather on such figures as physicians, architects, and engineers— all of whom, he recommended, would benefit from studying the ways in which apprenticeship models of learning are used in fields such as athletics, the arts, and craft groups. From Schön's initial work, models emerged for professional training that emphasized knowing-in-action and reflection-in-action. Significantly, in 1987, Schön himself delivered an address to the American Educational Research Association conference in Washington, D.C.—a talk whose title echoed that of his second major book, published that year, *Educating the Reflective Practitioner*. Schön's talk explicitly identified the field of education as a site where his program for reflection-centered learning could be applied, and he proposed "reflection-ON-reflection-in-action" as an important skill for teachers to develop—one requiring "verbalization and symbolization." Schon's 1987 talk is especially significant to our project for two reasons. First, the occasion of working together enabled teachers to articulate their reflections and other changes for shared "reflection-ON-reflection in action" in both oral and written texts. Second, these opportunities provided teachers with access to "symbolization" of teaching principles in their making of essays for other teacher readers.

Meanwhile, as teacher educators were paying increasing attention to Schön's model, both applications of his ideas and new compatible frameworks were being explored in a range of other professional contexts. Key leaders in organizational theory, such as Peter Senge, and scholars studying social learning, such as anthropologist Jean Lave and learning theorist Etienne Wenger, gradually built a body of knowledge leading to the concept of "communities of practice." As this research has noted, many communities of practice are informal learning groups, like the office-machine repair technicians described by Barry Sugarman—workers who might seem to be doing their jobs independently but who, in supportive organizational environments, might actually be sharing stories of their methods and experiences in unstructured yet highly productive ways—not unlike the teachers who talk in Patricia Lambert Stock's "The Function of Teacher Anecdote." As Mark Smith's recent overview of communities of practice has pointed out, these fluid, informal social learning units are actually all around us, and many people participate in several of them at any given time. And as Lave and Wenger have illustrated in studies of apprenticeships operating within communities of practice (e.g., servicemen, midwives, meat-cutters), new members of such groups can be gradually acculturated to enable their participation; doing so reshapes their identities, as well as provides access to shared skills.[2]

But communities of practice can also be organized more formally to support the learning processes associated with their goals. Interestingly, some formal educational institutions have resisted this possibility—either overtly through compartmentalized designs for teaching and learning or, indirectly, by failing to support informal communities of practice seeking to organize. However, a few professions have gone beyond simply allowing communities of practice to flourish to directly promoting careful analysis of how such work can support professionalization. At the fore of research on how such communities of practice (can) function through formal, structured learning has been the medical profession.

Atul Gawande's *Complications: A Surgeon's Notes on an Imperfect Science* exemplifies well how formal communities of practice work. In *Complications*, Atul Gawande, a seventh-year surgical resident, describes, dramatizes, and explicates the culture of medicine, particularly the community of practice inhabited by surgeons. Among the most interesting reflections informing the book is a consideration of how surgeons know what they know. Most of us perceive medicine as science, a discipline whose epistemology is located in control groups, protocols, treatment variables, and chi squares calculating significant differences. Gawande, however, complicates such a view. In addition to relying on quantifiable information, medicine, he says, relies on the human story: "In the end it is sometimes not science but what people tell us that is the most convincing proof we have" (207).

Although Gawande uses neither the word *reflection* nor the phrase *community of practice*, what he portrays is his own socialization into a community of surgeons who rely on reflection to inform and interrogate practice and to make knowledge, especially in the M & M, the weekly Morbidity and Mortality conference, held precisely so that surgeons can gather to review practice and to focus on errors in practice in order to understand their causes and in order to reduce the likelihood of their repeating. The protocol for the M & M never varies. The physician in charge speaks for the entire team, even if she or he wasn't present at the event under inquiry. In other words, a resident might have handled the case, but the person responsible (called, often ironically, the attending physician) speaks. First presented is information about the case: age of patient, reason for surgery, progress of surgery. Next the surgeon outlines what happened, focusing on the error in question. That there was an error is not in question, so the point is to see if that error might have been discerned more readily and thus to have produced a positive outcome. The surgeon provides an analysis and responds to questions; the surgeon continues to act as spokesperson for the entire medical team. The physician members of the team, regardless of rank, are included but do not speak; the other members of the medical team, including nurses and technicians, are excluded, as are patients. The presentation concludes with a directive about how such prototypic cases should be handled in the future.

Several assumptions relevant to our project undergird this community of practice. For one, while error is not considered acceptable, it is considered *normal;* accordingly, physicians aren't interested in linking the particular doctor to the error, but rather *the error to the practice*. This discourse, then, is optimistic, predicated on the idea that through the discourse, change and knowledge can be made. This emphasis on practice rather than agent is likewise reflected in the form the discourse takes. According to Gawande, "A successful M & M presentation inevitably involves a certain elision of detail and a lot of passive verbs. No one screws up a cricothyroidotomy. Instead, 'a cricothyroidotomy was attempted without success'" (59). Not least, the discourse also encourages the physician to inhabit an interesting intersection between self-doubt and blame. Temporarily, blame is acceptable, but once established, the physician has to shake it off. Self-doubt is continuous, but can't be allowed to be debilitating. According to Gawande, a surgeon who doesn't bring self-doubt and humility to the operating table—much, we might think, like a teacher bringing the same attitudes to the classroom—is losing the essence of being a surgeon.

In a number of ways, Gawande's account of professionalization within the medical profession has parallels with recent research on school environments that effectively promote teachers' professional growth. For example, in "The Insiders: Development in School with Colleagues Can Succeed," Margaret A. Johnson and Gregory A. Johnson describe characteristics of school settings that foster teachers' ability to manage their own professionalization by providing opportunities to talk together in an unfettered atmosphere, but at a regularly scheduled time using an agreed-upon framework somewhat similar to the Morbidity and Mortality conference shown by Gawande. Similarly, Ann Lieberman has echoed Gawande's account by offering a portrait of a successful elementary school where teachers managed their own professional development in "a true learning community" sponsoring organized discussions of practice in action (Sparks 53). Lieberman's and Diane Wood's *Inside the National Writing Project* points to similar effective processes of professionalization in the NWP.

In the model for teacher professionalization we offer here—one grounded in the social work of teachers' writing groups that are themselves nested inside a larger professional community—we find another related movement in the medical profession's use of "narrative medicine," a strategy encouraging physicians to write stories from their own practice. In "Sharing Stories: Narrative Medicine in an Evidence-Based World," David Hatem and Elizabeth Rider urge other medical professionals to join the "reflective practice" movement by writing stories grounded in reflection as well as observation, using social approaches to knowledge-building that simultaneously encourage "empathy, [additional] reflection, professionalism, and trust," all of which they associate with "narrative competence" (252).

Set in the context of professional development through reflection-oriented communities of practice, this book provides examples of teachers achieving enhanced professionalization by participating in small writing groups that were nested within a larger community of practice. Significantly different, however, from the learning of physicians participating in the M & M conferences in Gawande's account, the central feature of learning by members of this community of practice was *writing*—writing with an emphasis on *reflection*.

Given the multilayered dimensions through which our authors did their work, several productive approaches for reading this book are possible, including beginning with the essays themselves, each of which addresses questions particularly germane to a distinctive institutional context (e.g., a specific classroom or specific school, a professional development setting such as a National Writing Project site, or a graduate program). Taken individually, each of these core essays presents one teacher's knowledge-making, made possible through a collaborative analysis of experience. Thus, the essays themselves are artifacts of learning that speak to the social processes behind their composition. In addition, to illuminate the ways in which each teacher's contribution emerged from social interchange, each author, after the essay, describes how the particular writing group influenced both text and composing processes behind it. The authors also reflect on additional, transportable knowledge (often about writing itself or about teaching) which they acquired through the group's shared reflections.

To help other groups of teachers adapt our framework for collaborative professional development to their own situational contexts, we also highlight key approaches we used to manage our various writing groups. To underscore connections linking a specific group's work together, we have organized the essays in clusters, and we have included an introductory narrative at the beginning of each of these sections, with a brief history of that writing group's experience *as a group*. These prefatory pieces recount how each writing group developed protocols that simultaneously built community, shaped the essays, and fostered professionalization of group members. While the descriptions clarify how every group developed its own unique approaches for meeting, exchanging feedback between meetings, and moving toward their final products, the introductory narratives also indicate that all groups had in a common a belief system valuing collaboration, reflection, and writing as avenues to learning. Overall, readers will see connections between those community-wide shared beliefs and the particular practices groups implemented, even though there were notable differences in specific management strategies. Therefore, on a pragmatic level, by examining the commonalities and distinctions in the ways the various writing groups worked, readers will be able to identify strategies that can be used to manage their own writing groups. But readers will also come to understand that, rather than recommending a straightforward formula or set rules for action, we have identified several core principles for writing groups' successful collaboration—principles that can be enacted through a variety of specific techniques. On another level, in tracking the history of each writing group as it worked to become a unit, readers will also see notable traces of the larger inquiry community's approaches for teacher professionalization: creating and sustaining time for collaborative reflection, a major focus for Group One; connecting reflectively to others' knowledge to understand personal experience in the classroom better, a key aim for Group Two; and using social interaction to build trust and refine thinking, a central process for Group Three.

With this context in mind, readers eager to consider writing groups as an avenue for collaborative learning and readers who want to study how these particular writing groups functioned as sites of teachers' professional growth may want to move from this introduction to a close reading of the introductory pieces at the beginning of each group's section. When such a reader does shift to the essays themselves, connections between each group's collaborative approaches, as described in their section introduction, and the content of the essays will underscore how participating in the writing group shaped the teacher-author's thinking and learning. Along those lines, when read in the light of its retrospective introduction, the essays in Part One, as a unit, show how shared reflection in a writing group can lead us to better understand our evolving professional identities. Furthermore, by framing their stories in carefully tentative, still-open terms, this group's essays highlight a theme at the heart of their work—seeing their writing as a beginning point, parallel to the excitement of their shared early brainstorming. Along similar lines, the introduction to Part Two will help readers recognize those essays' common emphasis on learning by gathering resources from beyond the classroom, then situating that knowledge in a context open to shared reflections *with students*. In their emphasis on the classroom itself as a space where new experiments represent a desirable approach to teaching, these essays also celebrate a component of social knowledge-making that was crucial both to these authors' particular writings and to the entire inquiry community's agenda. This stance sees instruction and reflection as inextricably connected and instruction as inherently collaborative, making teachers and their students partners as learners, much as writers and their peer readers became partners generating texts in writing groups. Finally, in Group Three's essays, readers will recognize a shared theme of revision, consistent not only with the authors' topics on revising writing programs, but also with the stage where their texts seemed to be when our inquiry project began. Though further along initially in the crafting of their essays than the other two groups, because of having already drafted in previous writing group experiences, these authors all found there was still much knowledge to explore through careful revision of their work in response to new readers' input. Self-consciously linking writers to social revision, this group reported in one status-check reflection that "writing is never really finished." Just as we learn to seek continued growth in our professional selves, whatever our working situation, so this group learned that writing products, however thoughtfully prepared, still invite re-vision of text, revision of professional self.

With these cross-group distinctions in mind, readers who are looking for *models of reflective writing about teaching* may find the core essays themselves the most valuable dimension of our book. These essays include:

Essays by Writing Group One: Creating Our Professional Identities

Each essay in this section tells a story of reflection influencing everyday decision-making by teachers and, in the process, shaping our professional selves.

Deborah Kramb's essay, "The Balancing Act: A Play on Managing Our Lives," grew out of a desire to organize challenges she faced as a veteran educator striving to improve her teaching through graduate education and National Board Certification. Kramb found that juggling her multiple commitments, in the short run, distracted her from day-to-day teaching. However, in reflecting on her experiences while writing her essay with support from her group, Kramb came to a deeper appreciation of long-term professional growth.

Carol Harrell, author of "Writing Monster/Writing Mentor," sees her undergraduate course in composition pedagogy as a forum for the exchange of ideas between instructor and preservice teachers. Reviewing student writing created for the course, Harrell explains how studying her students' texts enriched her view of teachers as mentors—both in her own classroom and in the classrooms her preservice teachers will eventually lead.

In "Build It and They Will Learn: Portfolios Revisited," George Seaman discusses how he introduced student portfolios to his classroom. The essay focuses on three key characteristics Seaman found to be essential for creating an environment where student portfolios can thrive: providing for student ownership, treating students as individuals, and promoting reflection through writing. Like others who have implemented portfolios, Seaman discovered that his classroom role shifted to facilitator, changing his professional identity.

"Making Mentoring Visible," by Dede Yow, makes apparent the often overlooked but central place of mentoring in teaching. Mentoring, while formally recognized institutionally on all educational levels, is generally not compensated in time or payment, Yow points out. Paying particular attention to the university setting, Yow's chapter gives a voice to the mentoring that is inherent in all meaningful teaching relationships.

Essays by Writing Group Two: Looking Closely at Classroom Practices

Both of the essays by this writing group's members offer detailed examination of particular classroom innovations, set in the context of ongoing developments in humanities education that are compatible with writing as a vehicle for learning.

In "Sharing Journal Reflections of Inspiration and Remembrance in Holocaust Studies," Renee Kaplan describes a Holocaust unit she developed for an eighth-grade gifted class. An essential element in the unit was reflective writing in journals, an activity she did along with her students. Like the other members of her writing group, Kaplan realized how valuable reflection could be in documenting and promoting student understanding.

"'Seeing' Community: Visual Culture in College Composition," by Sarah Robbins and Linda Stewart, describes efforts to enhance students' study of local culture. While investigating their teaching in separate freshman composition classes, the authors were both part of a large team of educators funded by the National Endowment of Humanities to create curriculum for community studies. Having used visual culture as an avenue for researching community themselves, they carried these skills into their classrooms.

Essays by Writing Group Three: Designing Writing Programs

The three essays in this section come from an elementary school classroom, a high school English course, and a summer institute for teachers. While the essays were developed by investigating teaching in very different settings, all three seek to carry out ambitious program-level planning for writing instruction.

In "Picture This: Using Wordless Books to Teach Primary-Grade Writers," Victoria Walker describes a collaborative effort to promote primary students' narrative writing skills. Walker and a colleague developed a visual literacy approach to guide their young students to understand narrative structure. Reading wordless books, students learned to craft three-part picture narratives and to see themselves as authors. Walker, meanwhile, learned how studying her teaching practice systematically could enhance her curriculum.

Leslie Walker's "Re-envisioning the Writing Classroom" tracks her own development as a teacher of writing. Her growth begins as she reflects on her own high school experiences as a student writer. Walker continues her search by observing two very different teachers at work. She then re-views episodes from her own classroom to reflect on her practice and philosophy so as to reform her teaching.

"Writing Groups Revised: Coaches, Community and Craft in a Summer Institute" examines how one local National Writing Project site conducted a self-study to improve the quality of the writing groups used in its summer institute. Author Andy Smith, working with other teacher-leaders, identified weaknesses in the site's instructional model and then helped develop a new one. Smith's essay describes that process and reflects on its implications for his own teaching and for future programs at the Writing Project site.

Setting the Writing Groups in Context

As engaging pieces of writing in themselves, and through the accounts revisiting their preparation, these essays make an argument for supporting teachers' social networks of learning. This argument is demonstrated in action in "Reading Across Writing Groups," examples of response texts that teachers in our community of practice wrote after reading draft essays by project participants from outside their original writing groups. Our book's central argument is also reinforced by a multi-vocal report from several teachers (Zsa Boykin, Sandra Grant, Toby Emert, and Scott Smoot) who served as the "first readers" for our entire manuscript. When we asked this team to review our draft essays, we had in mind using their comments to support revision. But we also hoped that they might situate the learning processes of our larger community of practice in frameworks that could be useful to other educators. They achieved this aim as well, and, appropriately enough, they did so by forming another writing group of their own. Collaboratively recording their reactions to our text, this group has made it possible for later readers to see an example of teachers adapting our work. Along the way, these colleagues extended their own professional roles, including their ability to write for other teachers.

One point these respondents made to us is that other readers would appreciate a close look at the nuts-and-bolts implementation strategies we used to manage the community of practice in which our writing groups were operating. With that in mind, the final chapter in our book revisits our entire inquiry project chronologically. There we describe how our three small writing groups positioned themselves within a larger community support system, which this book's editors monitored and facilitated, partly by orchestrating reflection exercises in oral discussions and on paper. That closing chapter suggests that teachers who establish their own writing groups may want to position their work to capitalize on institutional resources—whether in their department or school, in a graduate program or a professional organization. We describe ways in which our own larger community of practice, while facilitating shared inquiry, simultaneously provided the writing groups' participants with a logistical support system and a source of additional knowledge. In addition, that chapter lays out important connections between our project's emphasis on reflection-based learning and central principles of the writing-to-learn movement, including work on private, semi-public, and published writing as a vehicle for knowledge making.

Endnotes

[1] Like Mary Renck Jalongo and her colleagues, we believe that "teachers' stories, these positive and negative personal accounts of our lives in classrooms, are central to the type of inquiry and reflection that lead to professional development and personal insight" (xvi). Like Anthony Petrosky, we have seen that teachers "create knowledge with language and within a particular educational discourse in response to the various kinds of open-ended problems they solve," and we agree that this process also contributes to teachers' sense of their professional identities, so that "they are also created as teachers and thinkers by the language they use" (25).

[2] See *Situated Learning: Legitimate Peripheral Participation* and *Communities of Practice: Learning, Meaning, and Identity.*

References

Gawande, Atul. *Complications: A Surgeon's Notes on an Imperfect Science.* New York: Metropolitan Books, 2002.

Hatem, David, and Elizabeth A. Rider. "Sharing Stories: Narrative Medicine in an Evidence-Based World." *Patient Education and Counseling* 54 (2004): 251-53.

Jalongo, Mary Renck, Joan P. Isenberg, and Gloria Gerbracht. *Teachers' Stories: From Personal Narrative to Professional Insight.* San Francisco: Jossey-Bass, 1995.

Johnson, Margaret A., and Gregory A. Johnson. "The Insiders: Development in School with Colleagues Can Succeed." *Journal of Staff Development* 20.4 (1999): 27-29.

Lave, Jean, and Etienne Wenger. *Situated Learning: Legitimate Peripheral Participation.* Cambridge: Cambridge UP, 1991.

Lieberman, Ann, and Diane Wood. *Inside the National Writing Project: Connecting Network Learning and Classroom Teaching.* New York: Teachers College Press, 2003.

Petrosky, Anthony. "Producing and Assessing Knowledge: Beginning to Understand Teachers' Knowledge Through the Work of Four Theorists." *Teachers Thinking, Teachers Knowing: Reflections on Literacy and Language Education.* Ed. Timothy Shanahan. Urbana: NCTE, 1994. 23-38.

Schön, Donald A. *Educating the Reflective Practitioner: Toward a New Design for Teaching and Learning in the Professions.* 2nd ed. San Francisco: Jossey-Bass, 1990.

---. "Educating the Reflective Practitioner." American Educational Research Association. Washington, D.C. 1987.

---. *The Reflective Practitioner: How Professionals Think in Action.* New York: Basic Books, 1983.

Senge, Peter. *The Fifth Discipline: The Art and Practice of the Learning Organization.* New York: Doubleday, 1990.

Smith, Mark K. "Communities of Practice." *The Encyclopaedia of Informal Education.* 2003. infed. 30 Jan. 2005 <http://www.infed.org/biblio/communities_of_practice.htm>.

Sparks, Dennis. "Interview with Ann Lieberman: Real-Life View: Here's What a True Learning Community Looks Like." *Journal of Staff Development* 20.4 (1999): 53-57.

Stock, Patricia Lambert. "The Function of Anecdote in Teacher Research." *English Education* 25 (1993): 173-87.

Sugarman, Barry. "The Learning Organization and Organizational Learning: New Roles for Workers, Managers, Trainers and Consultants." *Evaluating Corporate Training.* Ed. Steven R. Brown and Connie Seidner. Norwood: Kluwer Academic Publishing, 1997. Lesley University. 10 Jan. 1998 <http://www.lesley.edu/faculty/sugarman/loandtd.htm>.

Wenger, Etienne. *Communities of Practice: Learning, Meaning, and Identity.* Cambridge: Cambridge UP, 1999.

Part I

☙

Writing Group One:
Creating Our Professional Identities

The Gift of Time

Deborah Kramb, Carol Harrell, George Seaman, and Dede Yow

We first met in September 2002, a diverse collection of educators, seemingly with little in common except an interest in writing and curiosity about how the community we'd been invited to join would help us grow professionally. We all aspired to be better writers and teachers of writing. We had confidence in the Kennesaw Mountain Writing Project—the local NWP site that had assembled the larger inquiry community for this project and then divided us into small writing groups. But we didn't know each other yet. And we weren't sure we'd jell as a group.

We came from different instructional levels—elementary, secondary, and university. George had just completed his masters in professional writing, and he is a secondary English teacher. Dede and Carol are college professors. Dede, Carol, and George had subject areas or specialties, whereas Debby, an elementary teacher, is a generalist. This diversity of backgrounds worried us at first, but wound up making us strong, because we brought a variety of perspectives to the writing as it emerged, and we asked each other tough questions.

Our process was very slow. We were not only in different locations, but we also had miles—and traffic—between us in the greater Atlanta area. We joked in emails to each other about trailing the other writing groups. Our different teaching contexts made scheduling meetings difficult, and we lagged behind, individually, getting started on our drafts. We postponed a couple of get-togethers as we each struggled on our own to begin writing. Then an important small-group meeting was held one wintry evening, on a date when we'd promised to come, however brief and unformed our texts. We arrived with very incomplete drafts, nervous about our seeming lack of progress. We sat together, silent at first, passing our very rough pieces to each other to read, making notes to ourselves along the way. Slowly, palpably, the intellectual excitement in the room grew. What we were reading was thought-provoking—exciting even. We sensed we had worthwhile things to say to an audience that could cut across teaching levels, and we also realized we could help each other say it.

That evening, we also realized the importance of protected "face time" together. We had been exchanging emails for weeks, but it was only when we met in person as a writing group that the communal energy began to do its magic. While it was difficult to make that initial commitment to get started—

it was right before Christmas and we were all juggling family responsibilities with end-of-semester grading—once we trekked out in the cold to sit in Carol's office, we were so invigorated that we made time in busy schedules for more meetings: we wrote them on our calendars and we stuck to them.

As we studied each others' papers, we became aware of the bond of our professional identities as well as the common issues we addressed in our essays. From the intellectual connections in our work, trust emerged. Debby felt competent enough to comment on Dede's topic of mentoring since Debby had expertise and experience in mentoring. George's subject of portfolios in high school could be applied to elementary classrooms like Debby's or to Carol's college-level portfolios in teacher education. As we began tentative discussion of our drafts, we found out how much each of us valued good teaching and discovered that politics exist at every level. The common ground of our essays became our starting point for the writing group's work.

It was somewhere midway in our writing process, many months later, that all of us discovered how much the small group work was going to deepen and enrich our writing at a conceptual level, rather than simply address surface concerns such as style and sentence structure. We were able to give substantive comments to each other because we had come to know each others' thinking and goals. We didn't always agree philosophically, but the shared comments informed our reflective process. And what we gained was invaluable and completely unforeseen: a big-picture view on education from the primary level to the college level. And we each gained three good friends and colleagues.

This deep learning didn't come easily at first. It took time and patience. Our first couple of meetings ran way over the planned schedule. We needed some practice collaborating to refine our protocols. For example, at our start-up meeting, we each brought only one copy of our drafts and passed them around, but that approach made us hesitant to put margin notes on the papers, for fear of shaping someone else's reading. Also, it was sometimes tempting to speak up and ask the author a question, but we quickly saw how that broke others' concentration on the different essays they were reading. And by the time we began talking about a particular piece, it was hard for the first reader to re-focus on that essay. At later meetings, we brought multiple copies, and we would all read the same essay at the same time, then discuss it.

Those discussions were powerful, once we established the protocol that was right for our group. Typically, we would first take ten minutes or more to read silently, each of us quietly making margin notes—both questions and comments—on our individual copies. Then, we would go around our circle to talk about the essay, letting each reader ask questions. The writer responded orally to reader comments, and other group members, in turn, would add response. (Once we had all made oral comments on a particular essay, we passed our copies to the author to take home, where s/he could read additional margin notes and synthesize them.)

What came out over time, in a seemingly serendipitous manner, were the connections that each essay had with the others. As we provided responses, we often recounted experiences from our own teaching, experiences linked to the topics under discussion in the essay. Through that sharing, the written text (with its moves to logic and rationality) often gave way to the unwritten verbal texts we were making together—texts that were more conversational, more grounded in authentic, shared emotion. Our oral responses merged, gradually, and found their way into the essays and into a kind of meta-discourse of ongoing, shared learning based in our writing. Marginalia we put on each others' written texts turned to conversation, then to more writing, and at the same time to stronger emotional bonds of communal experience in our small group.

Along the way, we all benefited from the superimposed structure of the large group. However, what had initially seemed a weakness—our different levels and working in different places—became our greatest strength. Our personal and professional bonds were growing, and so were our essays. By our final small-group meeting, well beyond the time when the other groups had finished their revisions, we were fully vested in each other's writing. We were actually reflecting collaboratively—and often in unison. And by then we had moved from worrying about time to savoring our time together.

A lesson about time and group commitment, in fact, was perhaps the most important aspect of our learning about writing groups. Time needs to be truly dedicated to sharing, we discovered, and careful attention needs to be paid to the writing group itself. One thing that came to mean a lot to us was the feeling that time stopped when our group started. If we had to stay a bit later to work with one of the writers, then we stayed later. We didn't hurry our work. And if that meant that someone didn't get a review at that meeting, then we scheduled another get-together, or we let that person go first next time. Our "real world" is a place of constant hurry, we eventually admitted, but the writing group should not be. For people to be supported, we had to give each other the gift of time.

Everyone worked hard. We learned the power of deadlines. Knowing that the others in our group would come to a session with some writing prepared for shared review helped all of us move forward. In a writing group, we found that we could be kind to each other in what we said and how we said it, yet be intellectually rigorous at the same time. We held each others' feet to the fire, but with gentle language, being cheerleaders. In return, none of us wanted to let the others down. Even while striving to be kind, we learned to tell the truth to fellow group members. If someone felt a piece's tone was inappropriate, or that an essay section lacked specificity, or that the politics of an argument were troubling, we developed ways for saying so. Feedback could be both honest and kind at the same time, we came to understand. Having gotten to know each other as caring professionals, we became very comfortable with our process and knew we were not being judged; we knew that we would receive only constructive criticism. Thus, we were increasingly empowered to take risks with our writing, to let go of individual ownership, and to make major changes in our texts, however difficult it had been at first to do so.

As seemingly impossible as our work had seemed in the early stages, the more we drafted, the more text we had to show each other at every meeting, the easier the task became. Deleting and revising was easier than generating—especially because, through the struggle of generating, we had developed comfort within our group. Therefore, once we did approach final revision, our pride was a community one.

Our writing group experience enhanced our teaching as well as our writing. Fresh from the energy of the group's process, Dede engineered more conferences with her students and more peer sharing opportunities in class. Excited about the experience of working in a cross-level writing group, Carol collaborated with another college instructor to create overlaps in their syllabi, so students in a cohort graduate program would have more opportunities to collaborate, to see the content they were learning as cutting across normal course boundaries.

As a group, we are now comfortable offering advice to other teachers interested in forming a writing group. We think at least half of the meetings should be in person. We believe the meeting space itself is important—that it should be somewhere protected from interruptions so that the time for writing group work can be kept undisturbed. We would recommend establishing parameters for group discussion, such as agreeing to complete honesty delivered with kindness. We feel that deadlines are important and that honoring meeting dates and times is crucial. We also think it's helpful to set a group goal for each particular meeting—such as coming with a plan or (later) a full draft—and that, whatever the agreed-upon assignment, it should involve bringing some piece of written text that others can read. We also affirm the importance of conversation in the group process.

Teachers, all of us, have our wisdom about our work. Strong teachers are reflective, but reflection becomes even more powerful when we have an opportunity to share our reflections with other educators. Then our reflection can change our classrooms—can even change the teaching of others. When we work collaboratively in a writing group focused on teaching, that group may initially be just a refuge—a way to avoid isolation. But it becomes more. The topics we choose to write about are the message, but the group itself becomes the medium: through the writing group process, we are able to influence others to join us in being lifelong learners. And, along the way, we become true professionals.

The Balancing Act:
A Play on Managing Our Lives

Deborah Kramb
Chalker Elementary School

Setting the Stage:
Enter the teacher, somewhat successfully juggling four balls.

I have a favorite story. A grandmother once told it, I know. I don't think it was my grandmother although it could have been. This grandmother compared life to a juggling act. "You are juggling four balls," she reminded: "work, family, integrity and health. And it is important to realize that although three of these balls are glass and very easily broken, one is made of rubber and will bounce back if dropped. The rubber ball is work." These words of advice came to mind often in the last couple of years. It is such a simple thought and so very hard to act upon.

This narrative is a reflection on balancing everything I care about in my life and how writing helps me link different yet related demands. I think that many people find themselves in similar "balancing acts." In the succeeding sections of this essay I invite my readers to revisit with me the challenges of writing and reflecting upon the diverse endeavors of a very challenging year: my preparing materials for the national board portfolio, learning from watching lessons videotaped in my classroom, and writing for graduate school classes, as well as preparing meaningful lesson plans for my first grade class, and reflecting on my students' progress. In each case, reflection helped me think about the difficulties and successes of the endeavors. Finally, I will explain how I try to continue to integrate professional learning opportunities and reflective writing into my personal life and why.

I am a teacher, and one of the requirements for becoming a good teacher seems to be proficiency at juggling. We teachers are pulled from every direction: the students, the parents, the school system, the state, and now, more than ever, from the national level. Teachers have information, pressure, and opinions thrust upon them relentlessly and must make choices constantly. My own balancing pressure increased that year when I began a cohort program at the local university, working on a post-masters degree (or a sixth year, Educational Specialist degree). A cohort is a group of teachers working through a degree program together. We began with a "team building" weekend retreat to get to know each other and then met two evenings a week for classes. We also met daily for six weeks in the summer. The required classes were interwoven, and we constructed knowledge by reflecting on how what we learned affected what we did in the classroom. Whenever I try to explain the idea of a cohort to someone, it seems to be so clear that everything "goes together" and complements both my involvement in the school and work in the classroom. Why then did it feel so, well, tense?

The analogy of balancing never seemed so apt, though, as when I began work on the National Teaching Credential as part of the degree. I started enthusiastically, believing that work on the credential would improve my classroom teaching. After all, wasn't that the point? But frustration set in quickly. If I worked on lesson plans, I didn't have time to work on credential papers. If I worked on the credential, I didn't have time to work on my lesson plans. And when, for pity's sake, was I supposed to work on my cohort "stuff"? It has never been my style to teach "by the book," and I usually don't repeat activities year to year because each class has a unique personality. However, here I was, copying lessons I had done in the past. Was I compromising my integrity? I can say I enjoyed the challenge of the credential assignments—really! But, I didn't feel I was able to give all I would have liked to my cohort work, credential work, or my classroom that year. Thank heavens for my understanding family and a husband who learned to cook. I began to speculate: maybe this challenge was not a bad thing. Maybe I was learning a valuable lesson.

In the three acts and the curtain call of this essay's "play," which revisits a busy year combining graduate work and National Board Certification preparation with teaching and family life, I will reflect on my struggles and the strategies I used (with the help of my colleagues) to keep all the balls in the air at once. I hope my story will support other teachers who want to take on professional challenges similar to mine.

Act I
In the Classroom

Setting the stage: *Reflecting and writing about my teaching principles in the context of my National Board Portfolio involved consideration of my career in light of each National Board proposition.*

Teacher is pacing, talking to her mirror image

So, beginning with the first challenge! The National Board for Professional Teaching Standards (NBPTS) commissioned two comprehensive surveys in early 2001 to examine the impact of their assessment process on teachers.

While many positive and important findings emerged from the two surveys, three stand out:

- The National Board certification process is an excellent professional development experience
- National Board Certified Teachers say that the certification experience has had a strong effect on their teaching
- The certification process has had a positive effect on students and has led to positive interaction with teachers, administrators, and communities (NBPTS Validation Study).

A second study, The Accomplished Teaching Validation Study, conducted by a team of researchers based at the University of North Carolina at Greensboro, compared the teaching practices of National Board Certified Teachers with other teachers and compared samples of student work from classrooms of the two groups of teachers. This study, released by the National Board, found that National Board Certified Teachers significantly outperformed their peers who are not board certified on 11 of 13 key dimensions of teaching expertise (NBPTS Impact Survey). Based on this kind of information, striving for National Certification seemed to be worth taking on at this point in my teaching career. The National Board Certification Committee has issued a policy statement: What Teachers Should Know and Be Able to Do (www.nbpts.org). This statement identifies a professional consensus on core propositions that distinguish accomplished teaching practices. These are actions that teachers take to advance student achievement, but the propositions also incorporate the essential knowledge, skills, dispositions, and commitments that allow teachers to practice at a highly skilled level. There are only five. With this information in mind, I prepared to create my own national Board portfolio. My reflections on the propositions gave me a sense of achievement, and surely, I thought, I could abridge the process of preparing my portfolio by organizing my goals around these propositions. Below, I will revisit the reflection processes I used to address each of the National Board propositions and thus to begin to construct my portfolio.

The First proposition: Teachers are committed to students and their learning. Ironically, teaching is a learning process. I don't believe a good teacher is ever finished learning. Teaching is a challenging, ever-changing career. It is exhaustive and exhilarating. And I believe good teachers make a difference.

So, I reflect. I have had a varied career, with time spent in classrooms from Colorado to California to Georgia, and students who ranged from children of college-educated professionals to recent immigrants and third generation high school dropouts. My career has also spanned several educational "bandwagons" and survived numerous "policy" changes. I have experienced guiding my own three children through LD (Learning Disabled), Gifted, and ADDH (Attention Deficit/Hyperactivity) programs as well. I understand the importance of one teacher in a child's life, and I take my responsibility seriously.

My experience has taught me to watch out for those children who learn "differently." I believe all students can learn, and it is my challenge to find the key to teaching them. At the fall Open House, my talk to the parents emphasizes that I "begin where your children are and take them as far as they will go." The only set curriculum is the general guidelines provided by my district and state. Then, I make goals for individuals, based upon the general goals of the grade level, but not restricted by them. I spend a lot of time getting to know each child and continue to listen and monitor learning one-on-one throughout the year. I have found that a teacher can never expect too much from a child. I strive to be a mediator of students and their environment. Children want to learn, and I want to provide the means for them to learn. For example, a few years ago I taught a multi-age (kindergarten/first grade) class in a lower socio-economic area where several of my students were Spanish speakers with no prior school experience. Since there were fewer boundaries to the curriculum, many of the kindergarteners learned alongside the first graders. My best student at the end of the year was a bright five year-old who had come into the class speaking only Spanish. I could have written him off. I am awfully glad I didn't. He watched the other children and expected to do what they were doing. He wasn't restricted to doing "kindergarten/ESOL activities." Re-thinking this experience, I make it the centerpiece of my National Board writing on proposition one.

Second proposition: Teachers know the subjects they teach and how to teach those subjects to students. I think I enjoy teaching because I had such a good time when I was in school. Now my students and I learn together. We believe the world is a fascinating place, full of interesting elements. I don't have any favorite subjects, and I rarely repeat lessons because of the variety available and the differences in groups every year. Experience has also taught me to connect learning to prior knowledge. I ask young children to tell me what they know and then give them new knowledge based on what they know. Experience has taught me to allow students to construct learning based upon their prior knowledge. Since I am a primary teacher, I also spend a great deal of time and effort educating my students' parents, and I want them to feel we are a team working together for the success of their child. I realize as I write the reflections on these beliefs and practices that I can incorporate them into my National Board Portfolio.

Third Proposition: Teachers are responsible for managing and monitoring student learning. Ah, the management question! I have found acting is a big part of teaching. I enjoy entertaining my students and getting them to participate in lessons with me. I have dozens of "hooks" that help them remember and understand. I know I was a visual learner and a kinesthetic learner, so I make a point to incorporate movement and/or pictures and charts to reach different types of students. I consider ways of "picturing" this important part of my teaching in my National Board portfolio.

Fourth proposition: Teachers think systematically about their practice and learn from experience. I have decided children learn best when challenged. The harder children work on solving a problem, the more they understand the concepts. I like to see my students accept the responsibility of working through problems by themselves or with their peers. I expect them to be accountable, to do their best and to be responsible for their own successes. Hence, I spend most of my teaching time working with small groups or one-on-one. The students write in journals, individually learning at their own pace. I teach them to find a book that is "just right" for them and read it to me. I base what I teach on individual assessments as the children work. As I reflect on how important individualization is to my teaching, I realize I will need to exemplify this dimension of my teaching in student artifacts and my own analysis.

Fifth proposition: Teachers are members of learning communities. Teaching is learning so I spend a great deal of time listening to other teachers tell of their experiences, reading professional journals like *The Reading Teacher*, and authors like Donald Graves or Reggie Routman, searching for new ideas. I enjoy taking part in "focus" groups with other teachers of different grade levels, looking into different challenges in teaching. I take advantage of our school district's professional development opportunities, and I attained a sixth-year degree in teacher leadership after fifteen years of teaching. The cohort program was especially rewarding because of the dedication, variety, and enthusiasm of the participants. It affirms for me why I do what I do. And having discussions with teachers I admire opens my mind to alternative approaches to teaching objectives. I decide to talk about these networks in my portfolio.

Looking back on my preparation of the National Board portfolio, I see its benefits. Measuring myself against the National Board standards required me to think differently about my teaching. I conclude that teaching is learning, and learning is a challenge no matter how old you are. My past experience in educating children is building my philosophy and will create a strong foundation for my current and future teaching challenges. My written reflections, enshrined in an organized notebook, serve as a reminder when the busyness of daily life crowds out hard-learned lessons. The process helped me organize my philosophy and set my goals higher. Accomplishing National Board Certification assured me I was on the right track. I found the National Board standards have changed what we all think about teaching. They are written to guide teachers in their own work, inform parents and communities about what constitutes accomplished classroom practice, and instill teachers with the respect that comes from identifying, reaching toward, and meeting lofty standards. I am reaching. This ball is still in the air!

Act II

Setting the stage: Planning and writing about videotaped lessons in my classroom involved projecting student behavior based upon my experience with children and then reflecting on their learning from the prospective of an observer.

Teacher with videotaping camera

The National Board Process requires that teachers videotape themselves giving a lesson. Sounds easy enough. I mean, I knew that I would have to set the situation up carefully and probably bribe the children to behave, but I am confident enough to know that when I am "on" I can perform pretty well. The challenge of planning the lesson was exciting. However, I didn't anticipate camera problems or six-year-olds being intimidated by a microphone. I think we videotaped six times—obviously it isn't as straightforward as it seemed it would be.

My first lesson required combining a social studies objective with an art objective. In Social Studies lessons I strive to model social skills that are appropriate for this developmental level and that will help the children later function effectively as citizens. I also strive to create a democratic classroom. We gather regularly as a group for class meetings, write our own classroom rules, bring problems to discuss within the group, and the majority vote rules in many decisions. The children take their part seriously and make every effort to be very fair in their discussions.

Leading up to the lesson featured in the video, the class worked on projects in teams. I wanted the students to discover they needed to cooperate and to communicate with each other in order to get the projects done to their satisfaction. We had several discussions in class meetings about the "rules" needed for teamwork, and the class deliberated on how to avoid problems within the working group. First graders are moving from the self-centered, winner-takes-all personality of a five-year-old into a stage where peer relationships are more important. While still feeling strongly about fairness and right/wrong, first graders are beginning to understand the feelings of others.

The lesson goal was to create a school flag. I planned carefully, trying to anticipate possible pitfalls. Together we wrote and posted a working plan for our cooperative groups to follow. I stressed that the effort had to show cooperation and that the resulting final design had to reflect the consensus of the group.

In planning the lesson, I had to keep reminding myself of the overall instructional goals. The requirements were to combine social studies and art. Because I generally teach thematically, this request seemed reasonable at first. But the lesson seemed isolated and forced. Looking back, I think the "big picture" of the unit was lost because I put so much effort into the specific lesson that was to be videotaped. I regularly use art as part of my instruction, but my efforts to make sure I covered the art objectives forced the lesson to become stilted. On the positive side, this requirement taught me to think more critically about how I include art in my lessons. It forced me to think of art in a more serious way.

The lesson went well. The videotaping did not. I was surprised that the understanding of symbolism came so easily to first graders. "The cheetah paw prints say that we are fast learners!" "We put on a sun because we are so bright!" There was lots of noise and excitement in the room, and the words of the children were lost in the din. But the major problem was a glitch in the tape: it skipped, blacking out every few seconds. We did the lesson again with a slightly different twist—but the magic was lost. I never would have done the same lesson twice anyway, and now I know why.

I planned another lesson, got a better microphone, set up the cooperative groups, and tried again. Incorporating art objectives remained difficult for me. Watching the video, I learned a lot about the way I teach. I talk too much, I make funny faces, and I have certain expressions I use over and over. But I saw and heard good things too. While writing the required reflection for the National Board entry, I realized that the social studies objectives were difficult for first graders. But I determined that the practice with cooperative work had paid off. I found that the staged "discussion" never turned out as well as an impromptu discussion. And I found I didn't hear what the children were saying when I was worried about leading the discussion a certain way.

I worked on the second video incorporating math and science during a weather unit. Planning was easier, although having the second objective was still complicated. I think I wanted to give math and science equal billing, and that is impossible. In the reflective writing, I found I was leaning toward using math in a natural, meaningful way, but the emphasis on defining math objectives and making sure they were addressed stilted the lessons. When I teach inquiry science, I just want to teach science. I want the math to come in logically. Being forced to include math objectives put a damper on the lessons. But National Board writers have these objectives in mind for a reason. Perhaps I needed to look at those lessons from a different perspective. What is it that Piaget says—the feeling of disequilibria is needed in order to learn? (Woolfolk 53).

As I organized and packed the videotapes and written entries to send to the National Board, I realized what a powerful tool the process of writing and reflection had become for me. Teachers are not generally called on to reflect deeply on their practice. A principal rarely asks for reflections when he or she does evaluations. But the process of writing the reflections helped me think through what had happened, to see the process as an outsider. Writing also helped me realize where a lesson was really good and where it was not so good, helped me organize my thoughts, and helped me set goals. In the study that looked at the Impact of National Board Certification on teachers, eighty-three percent of National Board certified teachers said they have become more reflective about their teaching. One respondent commented, "One of the strongest points of Board Certification is the reflective nature of the process. You cannot go through the process without it affecting the way you look at and try to improve every aspect of your teaching" (The Impact of National Board Certification on Teachers: A survey of National Board Certified Teachers and Assessors 4). Sharing my reflections with my writing companions in my cohort also gave me perspective on what I was learning and provided thought-provoking insight and new ideas. Our "A-ha!" moments, struggles with meeting the objectives, and successes tied our experiences together, and we learned from each other. Research concurs. Among teachers who report a high sense of efficacy, who feel successful with students, it has been noticed that even if these teachers differ along a number of dimensions—age and experience, subject area, and even conceptions of pedagogy—all shared one characteristic: membership in some kind of a strong professional community (Grimmet 33). Working with a group of teachers from the cohort, reaching toward the goal of National Certification, gave me inspiration, validation, and encouragement.

Act III: Making Connections
The Conclusion?

Setting the stage: Suddenly, with reflection, writing for three different yet intertwined purposes, had a common thread—Eureka!

Teacher sitting surrounded by a partially constructed house

My cohort program philosophy is as follows: "The program is based upon the assumption that learning is a constructive process that builds on the knowledge and experience of the learner. Through an integrated approach that provides choices and opportunities for decision-making and dynamic group interactions, the program is constructed around academic givens, and participants will partner with faculty to shape the paths by which content is learned" (Program Description published by Georgia State University). Research shows growing evidence that collaborations, coalitions, and partnerships provide opportunities for teachers to develop a community of shared understanding that enriches their teaching while providing the intellectual and emotional stimulation necessary for enduring personal and professional growth and development. And joining informal groups, such as the multi-grade focus group I worked with at my school, helps teachers to develop stronger voices to represent perspectives, learn to exercise leadership among peers, and use firsthand experience to create new possibilities for students through collaborative work (Lieberman 194). Milbrey McLaughlin has found that successful teachers, without exception, single out their professional community as the source of their professional motivation (Senge 1995, 326). I see now that this philosophy can apply not only to my participation in the cohort program, but also to my own classroom and to teachers in workshops I have taught.

Upon reflection, I believe that learning is a constructive process with adults as well as children. This awareness has changed the way I approach teaching. When I have facilitated learning, I have been astonished by what children know, and I realize I have failed to take into account what adults know (or do not know). As a result of becoming aware of the constructivist philosophy, I have begun to allow choices and opportunities for decision-making in my classroom more than I have in the past, but I feel I can do more. I believe it is important that students know they have a say in what we study and how we go about it. I have tried to be flexible and let the students influence decisions that affect their daily lives, and I have been astonished at how clever their ideas are. Michael suggested we change class jobs each week rather than each day, so the student would have more practice and do the job better. Will brought in a tadpole he had caught and thought that we ought to learn about frogs and keep an observational journal about this tadpole. Laura suggested we keep the bird identification books over by the window. Jacob asked if some of the students could sketch the ants while out at recess. My students were taking charge of their own learning.

I have encouraged choices and opportunities for decision-making while working with a group of teachers, but I have had to push and shove them to accept the opportunities. Is this because they were not allowed choices when they were in school? I have become aware that sharing lessons is not enough to help other teachers improve their teaching. Sharing reflections and analysis is what helps teachers learn, and modeling accomplished teaching can be done when working with adults. More and more, I have dynamic group interactions with my students and enthusiastic discussions showing high interest. And, with the adults, there is the hint of passion when we talk about perhaps having the power to influence school policy. It is building.

Suddenly I realize the different strands (areas of study) of the cohort have melted together. It has become difficult to see where one began and another left off. I suppose that was really the goal. On the other hand, I can see the parts within the whole. I can see constructivism in my National Certification write-up. I can see a teacher-leadership influence in my ways of handling people. I know laws influence how we must behave, and I know a school must move together with a strong cohesive philosophy. I see the connections when I go to meetings about using computers in the classroom to "build" knowledge and experience. I see the connections when I define my philosophy of teaching. I see the connections when I make choices about what I am going to teach.

The process of reflecting on my teaching while working on national certification and discussing my thoughts and dilemmas with other professionals has helped me realize my classroom was more teacher-centered than I would like. As a result, I worked to change the way I obtain responses from students, allowing them to think more for themselves. I had a base of knowledge I didn't even realize I had until I began the process: how teachers reach children, how they work with parents, how they reach out into the community. I had taken these interactions for granted. To realize that I had this depth of knowledge that I didn't know I had was life-changing. The national board process gave me a new kind of respect and appreciation for teaching. This awareness and subsequent changes I made have had an impact on me, and on my students, forever. If there is a problem in the process, it is that the reflection is never done.

Solution: Time to think. Time to digest. Time to plan. Balance.

Curtain Call
Spotlight finds lone figure precariously juggling four balls on empty stage.

Time adds dimension to all experiences. For a year I was caught up in a balancing act with little time to stand back and really see where I was. The balls I juggled never fell, but my concentration was so intense I didn't notice the world around me. I was limited to the task at hand. I had forgotten that I am a person.

I passed the national boards, I was selected Teacher of the Year at my school, and when I was asked about my hobbies I had to say: "School IS my hobby." It sounded like a joke, but I realized it was true. Being a teacher is my identity. I spend most waking hours thinking about my students or lessons. I had forgotten the grandmotherly advice that in life I am juggling four balls: work, family, integrity and health. My family is waiting patiently for me to learn how to balance, and my body is telling me I need to pay attention to its care. Like any addiction, it will take some time to overcome this obsession.

Unexpectedly, my successes have made it harder to balance. My name has now been added to a new list—teacher leaders. New opportunities have arisen to use what I have learned to help others. I felt myself again looking at a future crowded with choices. But I have constructed a new philosophy out of the confusion of the past. When asked to contribute to a discussion group or work on a project, I consider the results in the light of the students. Will it help me help them? My participation in my graduate cohort and the writing group for this book encouraged me to verbalize my beliefs about teaching. Involvement with other professionals has encouraged me to clarify my teaching philosophy, which enables me to focus on what I know is good teaching. I will continue to integrate professional learning opportunities into my personal life when it benefits the children I teach but I will consider family commitments and activities outside of teaching as necessary to keeping me from growing tired and stale.

I also realize the importance of professional community. Ann Lieberman noted in an article on practices that support teacher development, that networks, collaborations, and partnerships provide teachers with professional learning communities that support changed teaching practices. McLaughlin has found that successful teachers, without exception, single out their professional communities as the source of their professional motivation. I continue to grow through contact with my "professional family." Involvement with my cohort members continues even after our graduation. We regularly call each other just to talk about teaching issues and to bounce ideas back and forth. My involvement with the National Writing Project gave me a second group of strong teacher leaders from a wider range of teaching experiences and levels. Our common interest in long-term, continuous learning with the support of colleagues is nurturing and supportive of my goals. Sustained contact with these professionals, whom I trust and admire, continues to stimulate and enrich my teaching.

I love being a teacher, but I am a better teacher when I come in refreshed, feeling loved, and healthy. I am also a better teacher when I can exchange ideas and observations with professional friends. Just as I set priorities in the classroom, I need to set priorities in my life. And I need to pause, so as to have the time and energy to reflect.

So far, I still haven't dropped a ball. Perhaps those who read this narrative will recognize themselves and do a bit of juggling!

Reflection

As a primary elementary teacher, I had little experience writing for an adult audience before joining this book's inquiry community, but I have always enjoyed writing for pleasure, and I had been working on my writing for several years when this project began. In 2000, I had applied for the National Writing Project summer institute at Kennesaw State. Learning with teachers from all grade levels during the institute opened a new world for me. Working together in this non-threatening environment, we came to trust each other and wrote from our hearts. We pored over each other's work in small groups and coached each other. My confidence grew. Despite a lack of time for writing once the school year began again, I kept in touch with the fellows from my institute "class" and grew in knowledge through active discussions via computer. My experience coincides with research which indicates that networks, coalitions, and partnerships provide opportunities for teachers to commit in small and large ways to topics that are of intrinsic value to them or that develop out of their work (Little and McLaughlin). And I found that engaging in this new professional opportunity put me into an exciting and powerful cycle: the more I learned, the more open to new possibilities I was, and the more I wanted to learn. My own experience matches observations made in articles on teacher development and professional learning (Grimmet).

Interestingly, much of the work on National Board Certification involves reflection on teaching—through writing! Having learned the art of working collaboratively during my time with the Writing Project institute, I was not intimidated by the National Board writing demands that were folded into a graduate program in which I enrolled soon after I affiliated with the Kennesaw Mountain Writing Project. After my positive experience with writing groups during the institute, I was at ease working with my classmates in my graduate school cohort as we prepared our National Board entries. We discussed, rewrote, coached each other, and learned from each other's writing. The cohort also required that we write "Benchmark" papers every semester and a "Capstone" project upon conclusion of the program. These were essentially reflections on what we had learned and how it influenced our teaching. About the middle of the program, I was feeling the frustration of juggling so many endeavors: graduate classes, National Board requirements, and writing papers, on top of the daily routine of a classroom teacher. Writing about this challenge for one of my Benchmark pieces made it more manageable. I felt I had more of a handle on the situation after working through the frustration in writing and sharing my reflections with members of my cohort. Realizing I am not the only teacher facing these challenges and knowing others are contemplating attempting National Certification, I was excited about sharing my observations and insights with others, so I eagerly volunteered when our NWP site leaders invited teachers to participate in a project that would assemble writing groups into an inquiry community whose members would also be studying the process of our work in those groups. I felt ready to share my writing with a larger professional audience beyond my graduate school cohort.

I planned to expand the mid-course Benchmark reflection I had written during my graduate program, and I looked forward to the opportunity to join a new collaborative team, since my past group learning experiences had been so positive. But the experience of this writing group turned out to be even better than I anticipated. Unexpectedly, writing this essay brought back the thoughts and insights I had had while writing the original Benchmark and allowed me to evaluate how my teaching had changed because of going through the process of the graduate work and national board certification. I realized I was thinking much more deeply about the process of learning going on in my classroom. This writing moved me forward in my growth as a teacher.

The writing group I joined for this project shaped my essay in significant ways. Being in a group with members from different grade levels was especially helpful since I was hoping to write for a broad audience of educators. My teammates were comfortable speaking up when they did not understand was I was trying to say in my initial drafts. They asked questions of genuine interest, coming from their different experiences and backgrounds. Because I am a primary elementary teacher, what I do in a lesson was sometimes confusing to my group members, who teach in college and high school. Often they were unaware of the developmental process of teaching reading and writing at my level.

And when my teammates read my writing and asked for clarification, I had to really think about what I meant to say. No pretty sounding words or clichés would do. "What exactly does 'constructivism' look like in a primary classroom?" they asked. "Do you really feel you can individualize during journal writing?" "How can a multi-grade discussion group of teachers help the teaching of writing?" I had to make them UNDERSTAND what I was saying—which meant I had to understand myself. Through this process of addressing my group's questions, I clarified my own thinking and refined my essay.

Challenging as this work could be, it was also very affirming. I learned that what I had to say was important and that my feelings and understandings were not unique to me, or even just to elementary teachers. This growing awareness built my confidence as a writer and an educational leader. I learned to value myself as a professional. I learned that no matter what age student I teach, there are many things I have in common with other teachers. This knowledge helped me see I could be successful in new areas beyond the primary classroom. I am now helping to lead a graduate school cohort, which will be together for 15 months. I am regularly drawing on my experience in our writing group. For example, having learned about the power of a risk-free environment, I know that it is important for these new graduate students to learn about each other, so they can respect each other and feel free to express their own beliefs without apprehension. So, I have arranged time for "team building" activities.

The collegial atmosphere of my writing group also gave me a new perspective on my classroom teaching, adding depth and understanding to my thinking. I now realize that effective teaching involves conscious reflection and deliberation concerning students and the curricula.

Reflective writing on teaching is now an important, regular part of my continuing professional growth. My writing facilitates documentation, student assessments, and classroom observations as well as helping me connect my current and past experiences. Written reflection is like a conversation with myself. Writing allows me to verbalize what I see happening in my classroom, something I often don't take time to do. I defend, question, organize, and clarify my thoughts in writing.

My writing group also helped change me as a learner. Now I do not feel comfortable working on my own. I value other people's opinions and inspirations. I need other people's feedback and encouragement. When we learn collaboratively, we are not isolated, shut off in rooms with closed doors. We all have the same goal— influencing others to join us in being lifelong learners.

References

Arbuckle, Margaret. "Triangle of Design, Circle of Culture." *Schools that Learn: A Fifth Discipline Fieldbook for Educators, Parents, and Everyone Who Cares About Education.* Ed. Peter Senge. New York: Doubleday, 2000: 325-41.

Graves, Donald. *A Fresh Look at Writing.* Portsmouth: Heinemann, 1994.

Grimmett, Peter P., and Jonathan Neufeld, ed. *Teacher Development and the Struggle for Authenticity: Professional Growth and Restructuring in the Context of Change.* New York: Teachers College Press, 1994.

"Impact of National Board Certification on Standards-Based Professional Development." *National Board for Professional Teaching Standards.* 2006. Oct. 2000 <http://www.nbpts.org/research>.

"The Impact of National Board Certification on Teachers: A Survey of National Board Certified Teachers and Assessors." *NBPT Research Report: Fall 2001*. 2001. 29 Sept. 2006 <http://www.nbpts.org/research>.

Lieberman, Ann. "Practices That Support Teacher Development: Transforming Conceptions of Professional Learning." *Teaching Learning: New Policies, New Practices*. Ed. Milbrey W. McLaughlin and Ida Oberman. New York: Teachers College Press, 1996. 185–193.

McLaughlin, Milbrey W. "Strategic Sites for Teachers' Professional Development." *Teacher Development and the Struggle for Authenticity: Professional Growth and Restructuring in the Context of Change*. Ed. Peter P. Grimmett and Jonathan Neufeld. New York: Teachers College Press, 1994. 31–35.

"NBCT Impact on Student Achievement and Performance." *National Board for Professional Teaching Standards*. 2006. Oct 2000 <http://www.nbpts.org/research/archive_2.cfm?catid=1>.

Routman, Reggie. *Transitions: From Literature to Literacy*. Portsmouth: Heinemann, 1988.

Senge, Peter, ed. *Schools that Learn: A Fifth Discipline Fieldbook for Educators, Parents, and Everyone Who Cares About Education*. New York: Doubleday, 2000.

Woolfolk, Anita. "A Comprehensive Theory about Thinking: The Work of Piaget." *Educational Psychology: Third Edition*. Englewood Cliffs: Prentice-Hall Inc., 1987. 50–65.

Writing Monster/Writing Mentor: Reading and Learning from Students' Stories of Writing

Carol P. Harrell
Kennesaw State University

In the university where I teach undergraduate students majoring in secondary English education, one required course is Principles of Teaching Writing. The purpose of the course is to prepare preservice teachers to be effective composition instructors at whatever secondary-school grade level they work. To reach that goal, the students and I explore developments in theory and pedagogy, and we consider the diverse backgrounds and needs of learners. We also explore ways to bring various print and nonprint texts into the classroom. We search for meaningful ways to integrate technology into a writing program, and, because we can't teach something we don't know or practice, we write. I allow students freedom of choice on a number of texts they write, but the Writing Journey is an assigned piece in which students trace their development as writers from their earliest memories to the writers they are when they begin the essay.

Originally, I included the Writing Journey in the course as a text through which students might consider themselves as writers and articulate how school experiences molded them into the writers they had become, both of which the exercise allows. But the richness of the students' tales and my cumulative reflections on the journeys have intensified the available options possible for this assignment. One unexpected but compelling outcome of the writing is that the students provide a window into their hearts when they tell their stories. As my students articulate the significance of writing in their lives, I'm privileged to hear their stories and thus learn about them in ways only writing allows. I hear about the first grader who successfully wrote his name after many failed attempts. I experience the pride of the student who won the writing contest in seventh grade, an especially poignant moment because the student's parents were locked in a divorce battle and writing was the only safe place during the evening hours. I share the pain of the young woman who suffers from an eating disorder but finds solace in writing about the anguish of the disease. And I discover in reading and learning the inner thoughts behind the printed names on the class roll that the student stories can effectively direct me when I make suggestions and guide individuals toward the teachers they will become.

But these discoveries were not clarified after reading just one set of Writing Journeys. After several semesters of reading, I found myself nodding when I heard another student tell me that writing was a way to define self, and I was no longer surprised when students pointed to the single teacher of writing who made a difference in their writing lives. However, when it was time to write with my group for this book project, and when I realized I wanted to write about discoveries I had made in these student narratives, I had no copies of Writing Journeys to use as data. Rather than give up on the topic, I e-mailed past classes requesting a copy of their Writing Journeys and explained that I wanted to reread them and then use my findings in a piece of writing. They kindly sent copies, but to extend my research, I also went to colleagues who were teaching Principles of Teaching Writing and asked if their students might share their Writing Journeys with me. Many of those students shared their texts with me, and in their stories, I found patterns that exactly mirrored my students'.

These Writing Journeys provided a way to know student writers, but additionally they have become a tool that informs my practice and ultimately my students' practice. After reading the writing stories over several semesters, and after re-reading a broad sample in preparation for this writing task, I have discovered patterns that offer insight into the importance of the teacher in the literacy journey—potentially informing writing practice—my students' and my own. In studying students' writing journeys, I've found several elements that enrich the definition of my role as a teacher of teachers. For some students, writing is a way to express thought—it's a way to define what's inside; it's a pathway in the process of self-definition; Kirby and Liner call this bringing out what's inside, and this kind of writing often occurs outside the classroom setting. As a writer, I've experienced that self-defining moment, but reflecting upon the significance of writing as a means for my students to express thought pointed out my neglect of this critical element in guiding future writing teachers. In the class, my focus has been on teaching writing as a process, including some discussion on the outlet writing provides, but not with a well-articulated path by which the discovery of self through writing can occur. My students and I focused on the day-to-day expectations of writing instruction: grammar can be taught within the context of authentic writing, and class time must be provided so students have time to create texts. The students and I talked about the power of writing to assist the author to express thought, but the discussion was in passing and did not dwell on the significance of the writing act as an integral part in the process of self-discovery and self-definition.

As often happens when we take time to listen to our students, I learned from them; through their Writing Journeys, my students taught me that they need time and support as they write from their heart, but they also taught me that the teacher is critically important in the development of the writer.

Student Voices

Although not part of the class objectives, the writing journeys revealed the significance of the writing act as a vehicle for self-definition and discovery. Laura, one of the students who articulates the way writing allowed her to discover self, says in her journey that, "Much of what I write seems to be from a deep place in my heart, and I am always afraid that people will think it is stupid or worthless. So, I keep everything to myself for now. It is enough of a consolation for me that I have it written down, but I am not ready to share that with anyone quite yet." When I read Laura's description of writing's significance in capturing her inner self, I was surprised. She is a student I thought I knew well; she's outgoing and talks easily in and out of class. She appears confident and she seems to share her thoughts and questions easily, but she explains that some of who she is remains hidden from the world. She needs writing to interact with that self, but that person, defined through writing, is private, not part of the public world, including school and school writing.

Another student, Kari, says that when she began writing poetry, "Sometimes the words on the paper made sense to the outside reader, [but] some of the words only made sense to me. But what mattered most at that time was that it was mine all mine, and no one could take that away from me." Like Laura, Kari writes for herself and does not connect the writing that defines and reflects self with school writing. Both demonstrate the importance of the written word as a means to represent inner thought, but each uses her writer self as audience and intuits that a school audience could strip away the personal definitive nature of the writing act.

And yet, Laura, who talked about writing as a means to private self discovery, extends the idea of self discovery when discussing her journal. Although most of her personal writing was for private introspection, Laura says that when she was 12, she and her mother began a shared journal that allowed them to exchange thoughts and feelings. "[T]his journal was the buffer that we both used to record the thoughts and the statements we couldn't quite put into words." For this student, like Kari, writing provided a way to place the interior conversation on paper, but unlike Kari, Laura shares portions of her personal writing with a limited audience.

I discovered, after reflecting on students' writing journeys, that beyond the need to define self and to make initial connections to others, writing provides writers with a way to escape from and come to terms with difficult day-to-day realities. For Lana, who "wrote herself through the grief process" after her brother's death, the act of writing provided a way to distance herself from the harsh reality of loss while gaining control of life's situations because "for a few moments [her] opinion mattered."

Kari wrote for herself and used writing as a means to "escape from [a] life that I was forced to endure day in and day out. I could escape deep inside myself to a place even those closest to me would never know existed." Another student, Martin, confronted his mother's devastating illness through writing, but his personal writing was done in school. "I needed to release what I felt, . . . [and] in my stories, nobody was ever abandoned or hurt. Little boys and girls did not have shattered homes and a mother who talked to imaginary friends and wrote scary letters from God knows where." Rather, he goes on to say, life's hurts could be soothed because "writing was an aspirin for the ache of life; . . . [it] became my firewall."

Certainly, not all students who describe their writing journey are so passionate about the role of writing in their lives, but for some, writing provides a way to make sense of and deal with life's difficulties. In reflecting on these students' stories, I found the significance of writing and a desire for time to write, both in and out of school, but curiously, I never talked to my students about my discoveries. As I look back, I suspect I had not fully articulated the importance of writing for self with support from the teacher; but as I continued reading and reflecting on writing journeys, a striking discovery was that almost all the students focused on an individual teacher who made a difference in how they perceived writing and themselves as writers. Rarely did students tell of the cumulative effects of writing teachers. Jana's freshman English teacher, for example, had the students read classic literature, but "the most shocking of all was that we wrote everyday, day in and day out. We did peer readings, small group discussions and individual conferences. For a young person who loved to…write, it was manna from heaven." Jana further says that the emphasis on time for writing allowed her to pursue writing when other English classes failed to do so, and she praises her teacher for providing direction in and time for writing.

Laura echoes the desire for writing instruction but goes on to say that the teacher who did not "water down anything" provided the environment for her to "realize the [importance] of [the writing] struggle." Nancy says that "enthusiastic high school teach[ing] significantly enhanced my love of [writing]," and Mari Anne says that her writing was inspired by a teacher who "awaken[ed] in [students] a passion for writing." These are encouraging words for those who teach writing because each of these writers was inspired by a teacher who provided time and support for students training as writers.

As would be expected, just as individual teachers engage student writers, they also discourage them. Linda makes this point clear when she says, "One negative comment from a teacher can overshadow dozens of positive comments." Another student, Jana, reiterates this point when she describes her experience in an advanced poetry writing class that her friends urged her to take because the teacher, they promised, was outstanding. Jana, who writes for herself and had one teacher who ignited her desire to write, explains her poetry writing classroom experience.

> I walked into class that first day, excitement driving my feet through the hallways, . . . bringing me to class thirty-minutes early. SHE was already there. After a moment she demanded, "Show me your portfolio of poetry," and began skimming through it.
>
> "This one," she proclaimed.
> "Yes," I sighed. "That is the best work I have ever done."
> "May I share it with the class?"
> "Yes, of course."
>
> I could feel wings of joy and anticipation beating at my heart. Pride filled my thoughts, and I began dreaming of what she might say about my work. After covering the preliminaries and giving us time to write, [the professor] reached for my poem and began to read.
>
> "This," she began, reaching into her pocket, "is a piece of crap. If you plan to write like this, Jana, I want you to get out of my class. You're not worth my time." I sat, horrified, as she struck the flint on her Bic lighter, setting my poem aflame, unceremoniously dumping my dreams into a gray metal trash can.

Fortunately, this harsh treatment did not occur during high school, for if it had, this student says she might never have returned to her writing, but because Jana is strong, she has continued writing, although she says that for a time, "I never wrote another poem." As the pain of the incident faded, Jana decided to return to school, this time to train to be a teacher, and, she says,

> a strange thing has happened. . . . I feel free to . . . write poetry, and share my writing again, including poetry. It's exciting and daring to pull out [old books], dust them off, and sink into a deep chair and remember why I have always loved to read

and write, why I have always wanted to teach. Reading and writing are the foundations of my spiritual home, and I, at last, have found my way back.

A teacher caused Jana to abandon writing for a season, but she is a writer, and she returned to writing. Jana's teacher caused no lasting damage, but she might have.

Martin, who wrote about his mother's illness, had a teacher who gave life to writing. He says, "middle school provided praise for my writing. I developed a voice that was resonant with pain yet unafraid to move forward. My teacher saw potential in me...and taught me as if I were her only student." Martin ends his writing journey by reflecting on how writing, inspired and supported by a special teacher, allowed him to find himself as an adult.

I was in an airport when the urge to write hit with such a force it took my breath away. The simple action of writing words and creating the dialogue with myself brought me back to myself. Writing has shown me the path on which to navigate my soul. It has provided me with a window to this world, a world I make better, I believe, because I write.

Connection to Reflection

In reflecting on these writing journeys, I've come to realize the significance of the writing act in defining lives. It acts as a vehicle for exploration of personal experience through internal analysis (Elbow), and it provides a way to regain some sense of control in a confusing world. I've also come to understand the significance of the teacher in the writing experience—often only one teacher rather than what I assumed would be the cumulative significance of many teachers.

Yet, while reviewing these journals as I talked with members of my writing group, I have also learned that neither reflection nor discoveries that result from reflection guarantee changed practice. And, I also realized, but only after reflecting with my group, that my process of teaching self-discovery mirrors my students' personal self-discovery. When we have support and guidance from an informed reader—the teacher in the case of my students, the informed writing group in the case of the practicing teacher we are open to discover what we might never see if left to navigate our writing process privately.

In graduate school I took a semester course on reflective practice, and I wholeheartedly embraced the concept and now guide my students to reflect on their developing practice. Methods students are required to examine and rebuild pedagogical choices based on discoveries made after analyzing and rethinking implemented units of instruction; but as I consider the reflective process I set up for them, I realize they work in teams, and they are accountable to each other and to me for reconsidering practice—a strategy I selected because I thought their reflective process would be more meaningful if they talked about and shared experiences. In contrast, when reflecting on the reality of my teaching process in conjunction with the writing group I worked with during the development of this chapter, I discovered that when I consider my day-to-day practice, I have no accountability measures in place to support—or demand—the restructuring of my practice. This disheartening finding motivated me to reread some texts I initially encountered in graduate school. Although specifically describing the reflective stance of the student teacher, Cinnamond and Zimpher spoke against my solitary reflection when they said that the reflective act requires "active dialogue with the various groups that exist within the context of the school as a social system" (59). This reflective process is not to be done alone, they say, but that's how I have engaged the process. Clandinin and Connelly say that we teachers must "move into another place on the professional knowledge landscape[; we] must leave the safe secrecy of the classroom and enter a public place on the landscape" (14). Again, the emphasis is on a process that requires input from and responsibility to other professionals.

We teachers complain of not having time or place for professional dialogue, but Clandinin and Connelly further urge us to find ways to make conversations occur when they say that "[d]ialogue with the other participants is necessary for appropriate understanding and reflection" (59). But, they also say, even when we force the conversation, we may not find a "hospitable place for telling teaching stories" (Clandinin and Connelly 14) because, as Trimmer points out, we may have "difficulty trusting stories about our teaching, since we do not trust them to 'convey knowledge'" (x). Although these observations are true, if we are to move our profession forward, we must begin trusting our reflections and stories, and I would add that if we want to mature as teachers, we must not simply reflect and tell stories alone or even in groups; we must hold each other accountable for improved practice—and a writing/reflecting group like the one I encountered while creating this text demanded that professional accountability. As these thoughts converge around the reflective process and community I encountered through my writing group, I've come to believe that my professional inaction, my unchanged practice—even though considered— was the result of working alone and being accountable to no one.

During the process of writing this text—a process that initially examined my students' writing for what it said about the teaching of writing but eventually led to community analysis of my teaching story and practice, leading to a recognition of how to improve my practice—I began a new stage in the development of my teaching: I started thinking of my practice in the same way I want students to think of theirs, which includes public analysis with public input in the redesign of curriculum. With input from the writing group, I found myself thinking differently about the Writing Journey texts students produce. I made some discoveries about student writing from the reading of many Writing Journeys, but when I was forced to explain my discoveries to others, I was also forced to do something about them. But, allowing students time to make these discoveries, which I had not done in the past, demands eliminating parts of the course. So I must ask myself—and fortunately, my writing group—what I might leave out when I teach the course again. As I consider that question, I am mindful that students may be wary of expressing personal experiences with the school audience, and I am not sure I know how to deal with that issue; but the dilemma becomes a shared quest when my writing group joins my reflective process, and finding a solution becomes a real possibility that might include writing groups where members are accountable to each other, a writing experience modeled after the one that has been instrumental in my self-discoveries.

I will probably be a better writing teacher because of my involvement with the writing/reflecting group. Additionally, my definition of reflection has changed—the process is not singular; rather, it involves a community and accountability to the community and eventually to future students. As part of a defined teaching community, I've come to trust my teaching stories, and I've learned that my students need to hear those stories; I must explore with students the importance of good writing instruction and of teaching possibilities that grow from work done with colleagues.

Reflection

My husband and I had friends visit recently. Anne and I raised our children at the same time, and now that they are grown, we spend hours sharing children stories. Our husbands talk of tractors and building shops with elaborate vacuum systems and space for wide screen televisions. Their children and ours went to the same elementary, middle, and for a year, the same high school, and then my family and I moved. Sometimes friends evaporate during that process, but not this couple. They came to our daughter's wedding; we went to their twenty-fifth anniversary party. When I try to explain to myself why these people have remained close, I can articulate a few reasons, but they don't capture the essence of our friendship. Likewise, when I try to describe the importance of working collaboratively, the attempt falls short of adequately explaining the significance of the process.

Outside the collaborative process, the writing of this piece would not have occurred. I am a speaker more than a writer; most of my publications come in the form of presentations—in front of an audience where I can immediately judge responses and adjust content and delivery according to perceived audience needs. As a student I was too often traumatized by a teacher's red pen to willingly submit at this stage in life, but writing in a reflective, collaborative environment has caught me unaware; the experience has provided the setting from which I've begun to overcome my writing insecurities, thus allowing and encouraging me to complete the writing process on paper rather than at the podium.

Once I signed on to the project that produced my writing, my small writing community has been a voice I could not cast aside, and as I have worked with them, I've come to depend on their feedback. Their honest interest in my research project has propelled me and given me confidence in my topic. I can see in their eyes, like I can see in my audience's eyes when I am at the podium, whether my work is moving properly, but I can also see their genuine concern when it is not, and I have grown—in this safe, professional environment— to desire their guidance when things aren't progressing well. When I initially wrote about my students' stories of school writing experiences, I wondered if they might be too personal to share. My writing group took my concerns seriously and acted as an informed audience guiding me to see the significance of the collective voice these students represented. In their responses I saw a genuine interest in assisting, so that as the group process unfolded, I found— to my great surprise—I coveted response and direction. I wanted to hear positive and negative comments so that I could improve both my piece and my writing, and I've come away from this reflective process wondering about the powerful nature of constructive feedback on the writer and on writing. Like my students who frequently found one teacher who made a difference in their writing, I've learned the significant influence a caring, informed voice can have on writing, and I am forever changed as a writer.

References

Cinnamond, Jeffrey H., and Nancy L. Zimpher. "Reflectivity as a Function of Community." *Encouraging Reflective Practice in Education: An Analysis of Issues and Programs.* Ed. Renee T. Clift, W. Robert Houston, and Marleen C. Pugach. New York: Teachers College Press, 1990. 57-72.

Clandinin, D. Jean, and F. Michael Connelly. *Teachers' Professional Knowledge Landscapes.* New York: Teachers College Press, 1995.

Clift, Renee T., W. Robert Houston, and Marleen C. Pugach, ed. *Encouraging Reflective Practice in Education.* New York: Teachers College Press, 1990.

Elbow, Peter. *Writing Without Teachers.* 2nd ed. New York: Oxford UP, 1998.

Kirby, Dan, Tom Liner, and Ruth Vinz. *Inside Out: Developmental Strategies for Teaching Writing.* Portsmouth: Boynton/Cook, 1988.

Trimmer, Joseph F., ed. *Narration as Knowledge: Tales of the Teaching Life.* Portsmouth: Boynton/Cook, 1997.

White, Brian, and Michael W. Smith. "Metaphors in English Education: Putting Things in Perspective." *English Education* 26 (1994): 157-176.

Build It and They Will Learn: Portfolios Revisited

George Seaman
Kell High School

While taking a graduate level education course in the Spring of 1999, I was asked to select a topic for a teacher research project. Immediately, I knew the topic I wanted to address—student portfolios. Since most of my other classes in the graduate program involved writing and composition theory, I had been exposed frequently in my readings to the idea of using portfolios as a more authentic assessment tool to measure student achievement. Also, many of these classes incorporated portfolios as part of the assessment process. However, these limited experiences did not provide me with the knowledge or confidence I would need to implement a portfolio program in my own classroom. Thus, this assignment gave me the perfect opportunity to learn more about the portfolio movement.

As I started my research, one of the books on my reading list discussed the environment of a portfolio classroom. I remember being very much intrigued by the contents of the chapter, and more specifically, by the environment associated with a portfolio classroom: students who take responsibility for their learning, teachers who serve more as mentors than as authority figures, and learning that is meaningful and measurable in student terms. Perhaps I was a bit disappointed because the reading did not offer a convenient list of "how to's" in starting a portfolio program; however, I was inspired by the idea that changing my practices and attitudes about assessment could also facilitate the development of a more academic and collegial atmosphere, that together, my students and I would work to build a portfolio classroom.

Which Came First, the Portfolio or the Environment?

I was ready to jump on the portfolio bandwagon, eager to see energized students engaged in dynamic learning activities that would be documented in our portfolios, but before I could start, I had one question: how do I begin to establish this environment that seemed a prerequisite to a portfolio classroom? It seemed that if I did not create a climate that placed students in the center of their learning, then the portfolio process itself would suffer. Instead, should I move forward first with the ideas I had developed about student portfolios and hope that the environment would soon follow? Four years later, after experimenting with and modifying various approaches to student portfolios, I am able to appreciate the paradoxical nature of the question and the obvious answer. Which comes first, the environment or the portfolio? The answer is, of course, both. And neither. I realize now that it would have been impossible simply to alter the learning environment needed to build effective student portfolios unless I was able to develop a portfolio plan that gave students a greater sense of ownership of their learning. Similarly, students would not have invested the time, energy, and resources necessary to create meaningful portfolio entries unless the environment of the classroom reinforced the idea that they were in charge of their own learning. Over time, in implementing and refining a portfolio program, I discovered that the environment and the portfolio work together, each one improving the quality of the other. I also came to the realization that the word "portfolio," when used in reference to an assessment tool, is as much about the process as it is the actual product. As I strove to identify the principles that characterized the classroom environment I was able to create with portfolios, three essential themes emerged that are central to this building process: student ownership, the student as individual, and reflection through writing. In essence, by implementing these principles in our day-to-day activities and interactions, I was able to use them as the cornerstones of the portfolio classroom.

Student Ownership

I realize now that if students are to have a genuine interest in their educational experience, they need to have a more active role in the process. If I expect my students to value and respect the time we spend in my class, then they need to believe that they are instrumental in building the environment that facilitates their learning and success. Therefore, a crucial component of the portfolio environment and my portfolio pedagogy is student ownership. One of the primary goals of my portfolio system is to get students more active in and aware of their learning processes and the activities we use to achieve and measure this learning. With portfolios, I came to realize that assessment is meaningless unless it communicates to students both their areas of growth and those areas that still need improvement. Like too many of my students, I believed that my assessment strategies were to be used primarily to compute a fair final grade. What I didn't realize, though, is that the final grade mattered little to students if they perceived that they had little or no control in deciding how this learning could be demonstrated. I also figured out that too many of my students placed too much emphasis on this final grade instead of on the actual learning that takes place during the semester.

I recognized early in the development of my portfolio program that students should include essays from past classes that we could use as benchmarks. This practice was described in most of the research articles I had read earlier. Now when I ask my students at the beginning of the term to locate these essays, I am no longer surprised when most students tell me that they are unable to do this. "Where are they?" I ask. "We throw them away" is the common response. Thus, students believe that the primary function of their writing is the letter grade it receives from the teacher. It has no value to them after the grade is given because it has served its purpose. As I explain my portfolio system to students, I tell them that the many and diverse artifacts we will produce during the semester are records of their growth, and therefore, vital components to the assessment process. As students compile their final portfolios at term's end, they have the opportunity to tell me what they've learned as documented in their portfolios. I am also asking students to become more responsible in tracking their progress, and as this responsibility matures in my students, they begin to value more the learning that is taking place and to see their work as accomplishments of this learning. Carole Ackerson Bertisch also comments on this change that results from portfolios: "The responsibility, therefore, shifts from teacher to student so that by the end of the year, students should be able to evaluate their own strengths and weaknesses and write about them" (55).

Another shift that has occurred in an attempt to increase the level of student ownership is my diminished presence in the classroom *as an authority figure*. However, this shift does not diminish the important role that a teacher must play in a portfolio classroom. Chancer states, "It is the teacher who sets in place the conditions and the structures for what will eventually become a portfolio culture" (90). I try to serve more as a mentor, working together with my students to establish meaningful learning objectives and activities and helping them to recognize and celebrate their growth. Initially, I was concerned that this shift would bring about more behavioral problems, and indeed, I still have students who make poor choices when exercising greater freedom in my class. However, because the portfolios give my students a greater sense of ownership in the classroom, most will eventually learn to appreciate the vital role that they play in creating our learning community; as members of this community, they seem more concerned in creating and sustaining an environment that will allow all members to contribute to our learning. In other words, students become responsible when they learn how to accept responsibility.

This shift in my classroom environment has allowed me to put aside the old podium I once used to hold my lecture notes, and the overhead projector now sits dormant in the corner of the room collecting dust. Instead, our class discussions will typically find me squeezed into a student desk alongside my students, allowing our conversations to develop spontaneously, unrehearsed, and unscripted. With this new approach, I never know exactly how and when the discussion will end, but this slight bit of uncertainty is well worth the interest and engagement my students show as they actively contribute to the learning taking place during our discussions. Most students also seem to appreciate the quality of these discussions. One student, Ashley, commented in her end-of-semester reflection:

> In the first few weeks of the semester, I was surprised at the lack of emphasis on the usual note taking many classes use to stamp the concepts into the student's head. Discussions, thought-provoking questions (that's right—not the questions that are copied out of the book), assignments on interpretation of the works, and personal reflections replaced those dull notes. I loved the way we were given the opportunity to draw our own conclusions about the meaning or significance of different works, and our ability to question our previous judgments and interpretations.

Certainly, Ashley is slightly advanced in her assessment of her learning experience; she focuses more on the process, and she has identified some of the key characteristics of the portfolio environment, namely an approach focused on student-centered activities and learning. She recognizes that there are multiple instructional models, and she has reflected on how the differences in those models affect her learning experience. Not all of my students are ready to assess the process of their learning, at least not as articulately as Ashley has—most focus primarily on what was learned—but giving them the opportunity to participate in student-centered learning activities prepares them to start making these observations.

The Student as an Individual

As I've tried to establish this sense of inclusive community in the class, I've also realized that students become more active in their learning when I get to know each of them as individuals. To be an effective mentor, I need to learn about the individual talents and interests of my students. As we learn about these individual strengths and abilities, we also learn that the classroom environment we are building is enriched by individuality and diverse points of view. So compared to the one-size-fits-all approach to student assessment (i.e., unit tests, finals, etc.), the portfolio system allows me to acknowledge my students as individuals, each with a different set of life experiences, each with varying levels of skills and different interests. Thus, the portfolio allows me to see more closely how each of my students has progressed over the semester and how each one has internalized and applied the various concepts and lessons to his or her own understanding. Hopefully, the final portfolio also allows my students to witness for themselves the learning that has taken place during the semester.

One way that I have tried to individualize this form of assessment is to allow students to develop their own personal plans of improvement (PPI) for grammar, mechanics, and usage. Using the results from a pre-test that we take early in the semester, each student develops a plan that will allow him or her to show improvement on the post-test at the end of the semester. Between the tests, we have several resource days when students have the opportunity to work on their areas of weakness. We call them resource days because students have access to a number of resources—writing books, supplementary materials, one-on-one conferences with me—that will assist them in learning the skills that are covered on the post-test. In order for students to develop a sense of ownership and responsibility, it is important for them to set goals for themselves and then to work towards the completion of those goals. This objective, I have found, works better with skills that can be quantified, so we use this method in working to improve areas that are measurable with test results.

Our resource-day activities yield another benefit: they allow me to recognize individual effort and to reward those students who have demonstrated positive work habits throughout the semester. This recognition is possible because students collect the work samples and reflections that are produced during our resource days and then submit these with their final portfolios. Therefore, when I ask students to reflect on their present grammar skills and to consider their post-test scores as one output of their efforts, they can also see the notes and exercises that were produced during resource days. When I ask students at the end of the semester to write their reflections on the resource-day experience, many do have positive things to say. However, many also comment on the possibility that less motivated students will choose to be less-than-productive during this very student-centered activity. This possibility certainly exists; however, I believe that perhaps some students, before they are able to learn the specifics of standard English, need to learn responsibility and the ways in which decisions have consequences. Those students who choose not to be productive on our resource days are usually presented with an unsatisfactory grade on the post-test, and the contents of their portfolios reveal to them, and to me, that they did not make good decisions on resource days. More important, perhaps, is that many of these students are willing to attribute their poor performances on the post-test to the bad decisions they made during resource days in their end-of-semester reflections.

On the other hand, there are students who enjoy the opportunity to establish goals for themselves and exercise the freedom given to them on our resource days. One student in my sophomore World Literature class, Janet, commented on this freedom in her last reflection: "It helps me feel more of an adult, sort of like my own boss." I want Janet, and all my students, to be in control when it comes to her learning. Janet's comment clearly shows that she has benefited from this shift in environment and that she appreciates the greater freedom and responsibility that results from my efforts to serve more as a mentor. Her statement also reinforces my belief that internal motivation serves as the best inspiration for authentic student learning.

Another component of my portfolio system that allows students to make the best of individual strengths and interests is the Self-Directed Inquiry (SDI). Prior to the shift in environment, I had assigned research activities to students, but typically I had provided a narrow range of curriculum-related topics. After completing my own self-directed study as part of my graduate studies, however, I realized that it was an effective learning experience because I was allowed to choose a topic that was meaningful to me—writing portfolios. Now when students complete their SDIs, *they* select a topic that relates somehow to our classroom studies, *they* become the "classroom expert" on the topic through research activities, and finally *they* present their information to the class in a student presentation. I stress to students that they should select a topic that is of interest to them already or a topic about which they would like to know more. Two topics that arose from our study of poetry last year included a look at the symbolic meanings of the components of the Korean flag, a topic selected by a Korean student, and an analysis of the emotional qualities associated with certain colors, a topic that worked well with our study of imagery. I could not have anticipated these two topics as areas of research before starting our poetry unit. However, these two topics had some special relevance for the student researchers, and consequently, all members of the class benefited from the knowledge each student added to the poetry unit and the enthusiasm present in each presentation.

For this assignment students are still engaged in activities that address traditional standards, such as research skills, oral delivery, and composition, but hopefully they are refining these skills in such a way that seems relevant and meaningful to them. Furthermore, this activity reinforces the notion that I am not the sole authority in the class and that each student possesses some knowledge and experience that can enhance the learning environment of the class. During student presentations I become a student in the audience, a learner who is benefiting from the contributions made by someone else in our learning community. Again, by diminishing my presence in the classroom as teacher, I give students the sense that this is not my classroom, but our classroom, and they are more likely to feel a sense of ownership in their educational experience.

Reflection Through Writing

One day in class my students and I were discussing the nature of the learning process. I recall one student in particular questioning why we write so many reflections in my class. So our discussion continued with more student questions and comments until the dialogue led all of us to the final question that seemed to answer the initial question: if you learn something but you aren't fully aware that you learned it, did you truly learn anything? This dialogue helped me to understand the valuable role that reflection plays during the learning and assessment processes.

The artifacts that make up my student portfolios are certainly important because they help my students to communicate *what* they have learned during a particular lesson or activity. The reflections that are written about these artifacts, however, are just as essential because they allow my students to analyze *how* they learned. They are now able to recognize attitudes or practices that may have helped or hindered the learning process or the production of the artifact; they are now able to see the connections between the prior knowledge that they brought to the learning experience and the new lessons learned; and they are now able to predict how this knowledge might be applied to future situations or experiences.

These reflective essays are also important because they open up the dialogue that allows us, the teacher and student, to consider more closely the learning that has been achieved and to analyze the thought process that enabled this learning. This understanding has helped me to better appreciate the purpose of the margin notes that I place on student essays: they are to keep up my end of the conversation and to continue the learning process for my students. Consequently, the nature and quality of these comments have changed. I find myself asking students many more questions about the development of their thoughts, and as students respond to these inquiries, in writing or through internal reflection, hopefully the dialogue continues.

Finally, because the reflections in the portfolios become the voices of my students, communicating to me in clear and thoughtful language the accomplishments of the semester, they generate another dialogue that allows me to reflect on the effectiveness of my teaching. As Galley suggests, "A reflective teacher needs many frames of reference to draw upon. By using multiple lenses, I see much more clearly what I have done for one student that I need to continue. But I also see what I need to do to make it even better" (7). Thus, the reflections and artifacts included in the portfolio provide important qualitative data on the learning experiences of the students. These reflections reveal to me how my students feel about the classroom environment we've built. I was thrilled to read the following comment in Theresa's end-of-semester reflection: "I have grown in writing by learning to be willing to make mistakes." Through this lens I received affirmation that our emphasis on brainstorming and revising and on our frequent workshop and peer editing sessions allowed Theresa to put the purpose of the grade in proper perspective. She realized that taking risks and making mistakes will inevitably lead to growth and progress. I also see that Theresa was willing to make mistakes because she no longer viewed me as the red-pen-wielding teacher ready to pounce on the first grammatical mistake I saw. The portfolio environment and my role as mentor allowed Theresa to take risks in her writing and to recognize the growth in her writing process.

Epilogue

I've come a long way since that research project four years ago. I now have a clearer picture of what I want to achieve through student portfolios, and I've developed many ideas and lessons that work to create a "portfolio environment" in my classroom. I now know that students not only need to be exposed to important writers and pieces of literature, but also to think about other seemingly peripheral factors (peripheral in the sense that they do not appear in curriculum guides) that will have as big an impact on the students' learning experience as the curriculum: the attitudes they hold about the institution of education, the inherent values that have shaped these attitudes, and the role they feel an education will play in their lives. As Callahan has noted, implementing portfolios, over time, can lead an instructor to "a portfolio-based philosophy of fostering literacy" that sets student learning in a larger educational context (120).

I've learned that students need to have trust in me as their teacher so that they are willing to attempt the challenges that I will present to them during the semester. Ironically, this trust does not result because they see me as an infallible authority on language and literature, but because they, or most anyway, come to realize that I care about their learning. The learning journey we embark on will be an empowering experience for all of us, so long as I resist the temptation to adopt the "coverage" mentality that forsakes quality learning experiences. Student portfolios and the environment of a portfolio classroom make my resistance to this temptation much stronger. Dudley seems to agree: "Portfolios provide the opportunity for reflection that might otherwise be missing from my classroom, as we move busily through the hours and days of a school year, always trying to fit more reading and writing into every class period. The creation of portfolios makes us stop, think, choose, and reflect, activities for which my students and I need to take time" (3).

In essence, I've learned that the process is so much more important than the product. This notion can certainly be a hard sell to students who realize their college placement will be partly determined by their grade point averages. Further, most parents seem concerned mostly about the test scores that are published regularly in the media, test scores that are used to compare schools within a district, districts within a state, or states across the country. Admittedly, I'm not sure if emphasizing the process over the product is better preparing my students for these standardized tests. The real danger, though, in students' placing too much emphasis on the product, or the grade, or the test score, is that they will never develop a true appreciation of learning for learning's sake. What motivation will they have to learn if the reward is taken away? What motivation will my students have as adults to value learning, to continue to grow intellectually, if they believe the true output of the learning process is a number?

Even though my experiences with student portfolios have led me to a deeper understanding and appreciation for what can be accomplished through assessment, I also acknowledge that many questions and challenges remain. I know that once I feel that I've developed a portfolio plan that will serve all of my students every year, I will have violated the key principles that I've identified here that serve to make the portfolios worthwhile. Indeed, a concern I had at the onset of this writing was that some might perceive these reflections as offering a blueprint to be followed by others in developing a portfolio plan for their own classrooms. This plan works for me, but as I continue to learn from the reflections of my students and my own observations, this plan is always subject to change. Elizabeth A. Herbert, principal at Crow Island School, echoes this idea after using portfolios with her students for ten years: "we realize that there is no best notion of what goes into a portfolio; rather, portfolios serve as a metaphor for our continued belief in the idea that children can play a major role in the assessment of their own learning" (2). After ten years, Herbert and her colleagues still acknowledge that a portfolio classroom must be dynamic so that it can meet the needs of all learners in the classroom. I've been using student portfolios only four years. And so, the process, the learning, the journey continues.

Reflection

Teaching and research are closely connected, especially for the reflective educator. Being reflective becomes more productive when you have the opportunity to share your thinking with other teachers, when research you are doing in your classroom has an audience eager to listen, respond, advise, and help refine your thinking.

As our writing group work got under way, I had just moved to a first-year school. I would be teaching in a new department, in a different room, with students from very different socioeconomic backgrounds. Also, I would be teaching a World Literature course for the first time. Trying to adjust to these changes would be challenging enough; writing about portfolios as I tried to transport this system from my old high school to a totally new setting would present another set of challenges.

I began my essay by discussing the importance of the environment in a portfolio classroom. As I worked through the early drafts of my chapter, I was using the word "environment" primarily to describe the intangible characteristics, or the atmosphere, of a learning site that creates a place where portfolios can be used to stimulate and enhance student achievement. As the school year and our project progressed, however, my writing group led me to see that "environment" also applies to the physical place that is the classroom. For example, in my old classroom I had file cabinets in the room to store student artifacts and a designated wall in the room to showcase student research projects. In other words, I was able to use this physical space of the classroom to help students achieve our portfolio goals. But now, in a new setting, these factors would be different. I was unable to secure a file cabinet for my student work, and the lack of technology in the new room made it more difficult for students to use Power Point for their research presentations.

As our small writing group began meeting, and when I was still trying to get acclimated to my new teaching situation, it seemed that these changes were having an adverse effect on me and my essay. "What is my focus?" I asked my peers. "Do I write about my experiences in my old school or the new school?" Dede, Carol, and Debby reminded me that the essay was not really about particular experiences or lessons, but about the larger philosophical objectives that were driving my portfolio program. This, they assured me, could be reinforced by the organizational plan of the essay. As I considered their feedback, I realized that three organizing principles which guided my portfolio program at my old school—student ownership, the student as individual, and reflection through writing—were transportable to my new context, because they are prerequisites for authentic student learning, regardless of the setting. The lessons and the curricula would change, students would change, and yes, even my pedagogy would change with new experiences. One thing that didn't change, though, was my commitment to student learning and the belief that using portfolios as the centerpiece of assessment would facilitate this learning.

Another comment made by my peers also helped me to see more clearly the focus of my essay. After reading my draft, all group members agreed that an important piece was missing from the writing—my students. "We see you in this essay," was the comment, "but we really don't see your students. You need to give them some voice. How does the portfolio experience affect them?" On the surface, this issue could be addressed easily enough. Since it was early December, I knew that I would be receiving my students' end-of-semester portfolios the next week. I had encouraged them to write about their learning experiences in the reflections that go into their portfolios, so I read these more closely, looking for those comments that addressed student portfolios or the classroom environment. I wouldn't have known to look for this material if my writing group hadn't suggested it.

The questions my colleagues asked about my students also allowed me to reconsider some of the more significant themes of the essay. They reminded me that this essay was not only about the portfolio system I had developed over the course of three years, but also about my students. They reminded me that the classroom environment I was trying to analyze in my writing is really a product of the interactions between me and my students. At my new school the student population was very different from the students at the old one. Thus, it was only natural that the classroom environment would also be different.

This realization helped me better to understand some of the frustrations I was encountering in the new school with my portfolio plan. In essence, I realized that some of my students were really struggling with the "student ownership" concept. As I reflected on the increased diversity of my student population and the lower socioeconomic area served by my new school, I realized why some of my students might be hesitant to accept some of this "ownership." Perhaps experience had taught them that the institution of education does not always treat different students equally and equitably. Perhaps they had experienced firsthand an ESOL program that was understaffed and underfunded. Perhaps they had also seen reports in the media that criticize standardized tests because of possible biases. These are issues that I must confront in class partly because I do not want my students to use these claims as excuses to justify failure or even a lack of interest in school. "You need to give them some voice," was the main comment I heard from my writing group. Now I see my portfolio system as an attempt to do just that—to give my students some voice in their educational experiences.

My group members' call to put my students more in the forefront of my writing certainly made the essay stronger. Having a group from such different backgrounds *responding positively to my work also provided great motivation to stay committed to the essay throughout the challenging writing process. Getting regular, positive feedback in a timely manner made it easier to stay on track, and it increased my confidence that I have something to offer the profession. Finding my thinking pushed also had an impact on my writing beyond this particular piece. I guess the word is "validated." I found my own professional writing voice.*

References

Bertisch, Carol Ackerson. "The Portfolio as an Assessment Tool." *Process and Portfolios in Writing Instruction*. Ed. Kent Gill. Urbana: NCTE, 1993. 54-59.

Callahan, Susan. "Portfolio Expectations: Possibilities and Limits." *Assessing Writing* 2.2 (1995): 117-151.

Chancer, Joni. "The Teacher's Role in Portfolio Assessment." *The Whole Story: Teachers Talk About Portfolios*. Ed. Mary Ann Smith and Jane Juska. Berkeley: NWP, 2001. 89-111.

Dudley, Martha. "When Bad Things Happen to Good Ideas." *English Journal* 90.6 (2001): 19-20.

Galley, Sharon Martens. "Portfolio as Mirror: Student and Teacher Learning Reflected Through the Standards." *Language Arts* 78 (2000): 121-127.

Herbert, Elizabeth A. "Lessons Learned About Student Portfolios." *Phi Delta Kappan* 79 (1998): 583-585.

Making Mentoring Visible

Dede Yow
Kennesaw State University

Although many people think of mentoring as a form of teaching, mentoring is actually quite distinctive in its goals, processes, and outcomes. It has currency in the world of the business executive, the professional football coach, the ecumenical leader, the community activist, the physician, and of course, the university administrator. The literature ranges widely from the Cliffs Notes of pop culture, *Coaching and Mentoring for Dummies*, to *The Journal of Higher Education*, which has published thirty-eight articles on this topic in the past twenty years. On the community level, projects and centers, such as the Harvard Mentoring Project, the National Mentoring Center, and The Tao Center of Human Performance and Mentoring exist for the sole purpose of advocating and funding mentoring in various social arenas. In public education, the K-12 level's recognition that mentoring helps retention has resulted in most states in the past fifteen years mandating mentoring programs for beginning teachers (Boreen, Johnson, Niday, Potts 7). Medical schools not only build formal mentoring into the intern's experience, but also evaluate the effectiveness systematically in their professional literature.

Mentoring is a kind of teaching. That fact is acknowledged by practitioners in all segments of society and by teachers and administrators on all educational levels. But what kind? The image that comes to mind is the white professional male shooting hoops with the inner city black teenager or the first-grade teacher bent over a table with a child adding up numbers. College and university recruitment brochures show a professor with a furrowed brow looking through a microscope with an eager and attentive student taking notes, or even two men in surgical garb conferring over a patient in a bed. The small liberal arts colleges show a group of students under a spreading oak focused on a central figure reading from a book. Conspicuous in its absence, though, is an image of two teachers or two professors engaged in conversation. We who teach in the university know that we talk frequently with our colleagues around the meeting table or at the photocopying machine or in the faculty lounge. While mentoring happens in these conversations, however, it is not formal and sustained mentoring. In fact, while mentoring may be formally recognized institutionally on all educational levels, it is generally not compensated in time or payment, however crucial it may be to professional health and growth and however beneficial it can be to the institution.

A comprehensive review of mentoring in public universities leads one to this conclusion:

> Mentoring between faculty members in such [public] universities is not prevalent. Where it occurs, it is mutually negotiated, primarily between persons of the same sex and between assistant and full professors. Because there are few women full professors, women may be mentored more frequently by men or by associate professors.
> (Sands, Parson, Duane 191)

The Sands study notes that "according to ecological theory, human relationships are developed in the context of person-environment exchanges.... Where mentoring exists, the ecology or climate of the organization as a whole and within constituent units would be such that giving and receiving guidance are embedded in the values and norms of the organization" (179-80).

Mentoring is that invisible yet central place in teaching. It occupies no visible space. The question I ask, then, is why college-level teachers give time and energy to an endeavor that does not make the radar screen on the tenure and promotion portfolio and merits but a sentence or two in annual review evaluations? My experience with mentoring is a story worth telling, I think, if I want to give visibility and a voice to the mentoring that is inherent in all teaching relationships *if they are meaningful.* By reading the literature through my personal experience and reading my own experience through the lens of scholarly thought and writing, I examine the value of a kind of teaching that has been under-documented and undervalued in even the most enlightened of professions. I draw, then, the conclusion that we in the professorate must make the commitment to change the system to support this work of mentoring that is crucial to the survival and success not only of women and minorities but also to the integrity and humanity of the profession as a whole.

The school where I teach, Kennesaw State University, is a public university enrolling over eighteen thousand students in 2005 and employing over one thousand faculty and staff. The university awarded undergraduate degrees to over two thousand students in 2003. We are a teaching rather than a research university, and the institution's commitment to the centrality of teaching in its varied forms is reflected in the category of professional activity: "Teaching, Supervising, and Mentoring." In 1984, two years after my arrival as a new assistant professor, the President created a Center for Excellence in Teaching and Learning (CETL), which today offers programs for faculty development, among them the "Reflective Practice of Teaching" and the "Scholarship of

Teaching and Learning." Faculty assemblies have heard such speakers as Parker Palmer, Lee Schulman, and the late Ernest Boyer. The institution, then, has afforded mentoring a "place" within the system. What has yet to happen, however, is providing the means by which faculty members are afforded both the essential time to mentor and the recognition within the tenure and promotion system to acknowledge and thereby award mentoring. We have the band and the dance floor, but it is empty at the present moment.

My own history with mentoring has been serendipitous, extensive, and profound. I have participated in and led programs sponsored by CETL, and in my fourth year at Kennesaw, I was selected by the President, Betty L. Siegel, to serve as her intern for the year. An attentive and wise mentor, she was a role model for mentoring in professional and interpersonal ways. Even before my year with the President, though, I had two formative years of mentoring with Arthur Dunning, assistant Vice-President for Academic Affairs, one of the first African-American administrators at a University System of Georgia institution. With Art's help, I drafted and revised my first portfolio for third-year review. Within my department, senior women faculty sought to include me in panel presentations and helped me with portfolio preparation for promotion. The mentoring I had early in my career was crucial to my success, and its source is not unusual, according to Shelley Park, who writes in her essay, "Research, Teaching, and Service: Why Shouldn't Women's Work Count?" that "women, as well as men of color, are given more 'opportunities' for service than white men." These groups, she notes, are "sought out by other women or minority members as positive role models" (54). I look at my mentors now— kind and caring people who continue to make distinctive and fine contributions to our profession—and I see that they were the first and lasting role models for me. I wanted to give back what I had been given, so I mentored informally until the early 90s when departments at Kennesaw began to pair new faculty with experienced faculty, and I became a mentor to two new women assistant professors. Since then, both have been tenured and promoted. I am in a position, then, to know that mentoring can redeem more than a day that is going badly—it can change the shape of a career.

Mentoring is indeed "embedded in the values and norms of [my] organization" (Sands, Parson, Duane 180). Yet while my work as a mentor was appreciated, when I was to serve as mentor to ten instructors with Master's degrees hired to teach general education courses in freshman composition and world literature, I was not offered a course release until Fall 2003. These new instructors were fortunate because they had a double support system. The director of composition was their "course content" mentor, a role assigned to this position in many universities. My role, though, was unique in that I not only had a course release for my work as mentor, but I was also designated by my chair as the faculty mentor. Mentoring had a visible space in my department, and my specified area was that of "socialization" or acculturation, a fitting role in part because I am experienced (and perhaps because I am female). My formal introduction to new faculty was in the department's orientation meeting of fall semester. Since I was on the search committee for six of the new instructors and the other four had been hired the previous year, I had a basis of knowledge from which to design the material I would use. I provided a description of our department's culture and a guide to strategies for teaching and survival with a list of resources not covered in the university orientation materials. To establish that I was a key and accessible resource, I made it clear that my office was open at any time; I wanted to confer with these new colleagues, and I had the time to do so. Within the next two months, I had an hour's meeting with each. What I learned in those meetings, and in subsequent contacts, was surprising and disturbing. As instructors without a terminal degree (the Ph.D.)—hired to teach in a general education program— they were positioned in the department in a way far different from that of the assistant professor Ph.D. hired in a specialty area. They were faced with figuring out what their position would be in an institution that had yet to codify their status and position. The first cohort group of four instructors headed into their third-year reviews with their job descriptions still in flux.

The scheduled (and unscheduled) meetings, which some of the women instructors called their therapy, were revelatory. While the women tended to talk at length on different occasions, the men would stop me in the hall for quick questions or send an e-mail with a query. In almost all instances, though, I discovered that the focus of our discussions was not balancing life and teaching, or research and teaching, or even figuring out the tenure and promotion system. It was how we treat one another every day—in the hall, in the bookstore, in the faculty lounge. While the ostensible reason for my scheduling sustained, individual time with each person was to check on the stability and well being of those new to life in this university, I heard right off that they did not need my help in establishing their goals for institutional service or the extent of their participation in the department meetings. What they needed was a listening ear and a navigational map of the various personalities they worked with daily. While it may be a firm grip on the obvious that work stress is at the top of the list for new faculty, the literature on faculty mentoring faculty—what little there is of it—finds that the stress only intensifies in the next five years. The process, then, means that acculturation to the life of the academy grows in angst. In my conversations with the new instructors, I heard that their work stress took form and had voice in the quotidian details of their work and outside-of-work lives. Yet central to the discussion with all but one of these faculty was finding their place in the structure of the university, more specifically of the department.

In a perceptive essay on organizational socialization, William Tierney tells some yet-unacknowledged truths. He claims there are modernist and postmodernist perspectives on how organizations structure acculturation. The modernist assumption is that socialization is a "process where people 'acquire' knowledge, ... and it is little more than a series of planned activities" (5). In opposition is the postmodernist view that culture is not simply "waiting 'out there' to be discovered and 'acquired' by new members.... Rather socialization involves a give-and-take where new individuals make sense of an organization through their own unique backgrounds and the current contexts in which the organization resides" (6). Certainly mentoring, as the institution conceives it, propounds the modernist view that new members will be assimilated into the prevailing culture, acquire the means to succeed in that culture, and happily ascend the designated ranks of academia. But what I was hearing from new faculty had less to do with the organization's expectations and more to do with their frustrations and disappointments in finding an identity in the department. They felt "talked at" and overloaded with information in the composition meetings. They expected a community to develop out of their shared enterprises as writing teachers; they wanted to be acknowledged by their colleagues as fellow professionals. In one instance an intelligent and energetic instructor who had worked part time for three years as a faculty member before being hired full time was rebuffed on several occasions by a senior faculty member. She had expected to join the conversation of the department, and she was bemused by her colleague's treatment. While this story has a happy ending—the instructor and another senior faculty member teamed up to do classroom research—stories like these (and their number is not small) often have no place for their telling, and as a result, new faculty experience further disconnection from their colleagues emotionally and intellectually.

The truth is that we as human beings value the social and intellectual exchange we have with fellow workers, and this exchange, when tempered and kind, provides a resource that nourishes us and gives us a perspective when we need it. Collegiality, a concept that crops up over and over in literature about mentoring, in promotion and tenure guidelines, and in jest about the more scrofulous and odd of the professorate, is a real and viable force in our professional lives. Mentoring—in its invisible space—is the place where meaningful exchanges take place that can affect the career of a beginning faculty member. Yet the structure, as it currently exists, does not allow mentoring to have a central and visible place in public universities, even in those areas that house the humanities. The reasons for the continuing silence and invisibility of this area of teaching are myriad and complex. A compelling argument considers the perspective of gender in framing the issue. Once again I quote from Shelley Park's essay:

> Women (and minority) faculty are more likely to devote time to service activities insofar as they are more likely than white men to perceive the need for change in the policies, procedures, and institutional structure of the university.... They may also freely devote time to mentoring their more junior colleagues.... In 1989-90, for example, 86 percent of women cited collegiality as professionally important, whereas only 52 percent viewed engaging in research as important.... The notion that female faculty should cut back on their teaching and service work in order to devote more time to their research makes sense only if one prioritizes women's individual efforts to advance within the system over women's collective efforts to transform prevailing norms and practices. It thus ignores the fact that faculty women may feel a responsibility to, and a compassion for, both their female colleagues and their female students, in addition to women outside the academy. (59)

My own experience has been that even when an institution endorses mentoring as a valuable kind of teaching, the prevailing culture of the academy fails to acknowledge and reward it in any sustained and identifiable way. As one of the triumvirate of "Teaching, Scholarship, and Service," mentoring, and consequently supervision, which are largely relegated to women faculty, are not acknowledged in the area of service but rather are relegated to sub-categories of teaching. If an institution subscribes to valuing the scholarship of teaching, then research in this area may count, but if scholarship is constricted by discipline, then writing about mentoring will not be considered a legitimate scholarly activity.

My formal position as faculty mentor was terminated after just one semester because of budget constraints. A growing student population and shrinking funds demanded that I return to the general-education classroom. The abrupt ending to my formal mentoring relationship with the instructors, I realize now, did not give me the opportunity to move into what I have been doing while writing this essay—reflection. While I kept in contact with most of them, it was neither systematic nor sustained. I did work closely with three as they wrote first drafts of narratives for their annual review with the department chair, and I gave a workshop for four instructors preparing portfolios for institutional review in their third year. Inherent in the exercise of these reviews and the creation of a professional portfolio is self-reflection—*through writing*. As reader/editor I posed questions that asked for reflection and re-evaluation. These conversations served to give some closure to our mentoring relationship as well as to their first year in the department. During the summers, I continue to read portfolio narratives for junior colleagues who will be reviewed the following year, and as the department grows, the need grows. I have other projects to work on, but still I am committed to mentoring faculty who ask me for help. This inquiry topic, I realize, bears continual and sustained investigation.

Why, then, do I continue in this work that has no visible place or tangible reward in my workplace? Because I, like many, see my professional identity in mentoring. My agenda is both personal and political since gender does matter. I believe that "one of the primary barriers to success for female faculty is the 'lack of a supportive, even hospitable, climate'" (Park 60). More to the point, I have evidence in more than twenty years of experience in the university that women, when they have been mentored, are advised to give their time to research. Like Park, I think that

> advising women to refuse anything more than minimal teaching and service responsibilities in order to pursue their research arises from a masculine perspective that mirrors sexist attitudes outside the academy. Such advice assumes that . . . teaching, advising, mentoring, and nurturing students . . . are unimportant, uncreative, and unchallenging tasks. (74-75)

How I conceive of myself as a mentor in my particular university environment gives me insight into my own choices and how they resonant in a larger context. I recall a "Mentor Motivation Checklist" in *The Mentor's Guide* that asks for a yes or no answer to these "reasons that mentoring appeals to me":

> I like the feeling of having others seek me out for advice or guidance. I find that helping others learn is personally rewarding. I have specific knowledge that I want to pass on to others. I enjoy collaborative learning. I find working with others who are different from me to be energizing. I look for opportunities to further my own growth. (Zachary 69)

Shouldn't every teacher answer "yes" to all of the above? Wouldn't just about any white-collar worker? Or any conscientious Wal-Mart employee? Political agenda is embedded in every reason, but nowhere is the *structure*—which is determined by those in power—defined or addressed. My belief is that teachers can change the structure—that we have no choice if we want humanity—all of it, including Bartleby—to benefit. Mentors of all sorts can "facilitate effective learning relationships" and guide and reflect and coach. But I want more than that. I want a structure based on collegiality and fairness, one that does not tolerate unkindness (courtesy is essential in a civilized culture) or injustice. I hold these truths, and as a teacher of literature, I endorse and promote them in my classroom. I intend to extend my classroom and act upon my beliefs. My institution endorses the rhetoric. My immediate administrators gave space and a voice to mentoring, even if it was for just a semester. There is acknowledgement here, where I am, that mentoring as teaching is a worthwhile human endeavor. I quote Parker Palmer who writes that "Mentors and apprentices are partners in an ancient human dance, and one of teaching's great rewards is the daily chance it gives us to get back on the dance floor. It is the dance of the spiraling generations, in which the old empower the young with their experience and the young empower the old with new life, reweaving the fabric of the human community as they touch and turn" (25). It is why I became a teacher in the first place: to join the archetypal dance. Finally, I believe that all of us in this profession of teaching have no choice. We must commit to this common cause of our humanity. We must join the dance.

Reflection

My mentoring assignment began about the same time as my involvement in our teacher inquiry community. I was given, for that fall semester, a course reassignment in my department to serve as mentor for six newly hired instructors and four instructors hired the previous year. A year earlier I had petitioned my chair for the reassigned time necessary for this absolutely crucial work of mentoring. In the spirit of the times, budget would not allow it. But this time I had done my homework: during the annual review with my department chair, I presented how little research had been done on faculty mentoring faculty in the university. I proposed a design in practical what-I-would-do terms. So, granted the time I needed, my year began with promise.

I saw my new engagement with teaching as full of potential in the scholarship of teaching arena. Since I had been informally mentoring for over ten years, I figured the luxury of time and endorsement of the institution would afford me the leisure of reflection and the means to document my reflections and my experience. Thus, when I joined this book project's team, my topic was evident from the first: my writing would center on mentoring my instructor colleagues. I would have a chance to define mentoring, query how it differs from classroom teaching and conferencing and, most important to me, find out why I had for so long given my time and energy to an endeavor that had no visible rewards. Here was my perfect laboratory.

But by the time our inquiry community started meeting, I had already encountered many constraints in my efforts to serve as a collegial mentor. Therefore, my first draft revealed my own disillusionment and the anger that was obscuring any analysis I intended. I took very brief notes to the fall workshop of the whole inquiry community. We met first in the large-group setting with directed writing and intensive discussion of our overarching project questions. Then our small writing group read and annotated each other's pieces. George and Debby seemed pretty far along; Carol and I were still sketching, but at least Carol had a clear focus and outline.

Our next writing group get-together was in December. On a dreary and cold day, we met in the late afternoon. I admit that I approached the task with a tired resignation; I had a stack of final exams that I needed to read and return, and my mindset was grim—just get it done, I thought. Instead, I realized connections I had not made before: Debby's and Carol's and George's topics touched on mine in a very real way. Managing one's life, keeping all the balls in the air: this dilemma of Debby's was central in every conversation I had had so far in my mentoring the instructors. Building a community of trust and cooperation in a portfolio classroom—George's goal—was a central concern of instructors who had been teaching for a few years and were now growing into reflective practitioners. Carol too was examining mentoring—how to lead preservice teachers toward productive teaching models. Through our conversation, I had the revelation that my subject—mentoring—was something each member of our group cared about. Two of my colleagues gave me examples of applied mentoring that helped push my thinking. In addition, Debby had done research on mentoring in graduate programs, and she shared that information with me.

It was more than the conjunction of the topics we were writing on that jolted me that gray afternoon, however. It was the process that I saw Debby and George and Carol working through in their drafts and revision. They startled me with their sheer honesty about the conflicts in their teaching settings—different from, yet so similar to my own. Their studied restructuring to clarify their ideas was a sharp contrast to my six (yes, still only six) pages consisting solely of grievances punctuated with anecdotes. My thinly veiled anger at what I saw as injustices in several institutional arenas was neither reflective nor very professional. My group let me talk through my anger, though. They listened to my frustration with the lack of recognition in my workplace for peer mentoring, and this "group therapy" moved me intellectually toward more scholarly investigation. Caught up in the emotion of my politics, I had forgotten my audience. I had forgotten how alienating anger is and how tedious preaching is. My group helped me get the emotion out and then draft beyond it.

Through their questions and stories, I saw that I was reacting, not reflecting, and in reading the models of their writing, I realized I had a long way to go.

I began by tempering my approach. I went back to my research into the topic of mentoring in higher education. Having merely glanced at the scholarship before, I was now looking closely and critically. My results were revelatory.

In the months that followed, and through numerous meetings, I learned to draft, draft, draft. I learned to let go of sentences I adored and paragraphs I prized. I learned to open up to criticism that was directed at my ideas, not at my emotional responses to my situation. I learned that I have to get to the issues and ideas through writing, and then refine them in more drafting. Once revision refined my thinking, I could combine head and heart in prose that flowed and, I hoped, persuaded.

Meanwhile, my writing group's talk about how energizing and productive their work was with their colleagues opened my eyes to my own alienation and helped me focus instead on the possibilities inherent in my own situation. Together we acknowledged that mentoring was nominally recognized though not always compensated. Teaching is a form of mentoring, and conversely mentoring means teaching.

Through the mentoring of my small group, I moved beyond the disappointment and defeat shadowing that early draft of my paper to an enlightened, analytical view of mentoring in teaching. While I thought I had cleared my own political agenda, I had not. I had to examine my own motives for drafting a screed narrating isolated incidents in a department under stress in a time of great growth and shrinking budget. My colleagues helped me to channel my righteous indignation. My group gave me a perspective on the tone of voice in my writing. They wanted me to focus, not on me, but on how the system could be changed, and so my shift in direction resulted in a change in tone and in my truly finding a voice and hope. The hope spurred me to research and to read, and my succeeding drafts moved to a tone of inquiry. As a result, my writing gained a clarity that would give visibility and a voice to my topic.

And so my essay did a complete turn. Mentoring and its place in university culture were now my overriding concerns. I questioned whether mentoring in the university—if it occurred outside the classroom—was validated within the profession. I realized my group was mentoring me by holding up for me that mirror I had so many times held up for my students, one that I was now holding up for my new colleagues whom I was mentoring. As I recorded my group's perspectives, I saw once again the truth of what we tell our students: writing down makes clear what we think. I set up a series of questions for myself, beginning with "In a mentoring process, can feedback from a sympathetic colleague provide the shift in perspective necessary for clear seeing and clear thinking?"

Reflection had grown into a series of questions that I wanted to address. Only then did I move forward to articulate my own dilemma as one within the teaching profession: how to make visible the mentoring that is inherent in all teaching relationships *if they are meaningful*. This space is yet to be named; we call it the "interpersonal" area. It doesn't carry the rant and rhetoric of politics because its outpost is the heart. That's what I came to write about, because I now had a hopeful reason to write. I had an audience who cared. I had compassionate human faces in my mind when I researched and wrote and revised.

Our regular meetings ran more than a year. In fact, we continued meeting into a second fall, four months after other groups had finished their first round of revisions: we were the late bloomers, the long marchers. I look back over that year and a half working with George and Debby and Carol, and I see how their experiences had engaged me, and at the risk of being sentimental, how our conversations lifted my spirits and took me back to a place of vision and hope, away from the cynicism that had slowly crept into my view of my profession.

We are all afraid to show what we write in early stages. The more we draft and show, however, the easier it becomes to strip away the unnecessary and to refine. And once that final revision is before a writing group, the pride is a community one. That's the graduation dance, the best one of all.

References

Boreen, Jean, Mary K. Johnson, Donna Niday, and Joe Potts. *Mentoring Beginning Teachers: Guiding, Reflecting, Coaching*. York: Stenhouse, 2000.

Palmer, Parker J. *The Courage to Teach: Exploring the Inner Landscape of a Teacher's Life*. San Francisco: Jossey-Bass, 1998.

Park, Shelley M. "Research, Teaching, and Service: Why Shouldn't Women's Work Count?" *The Journal of Higher Education* 67 (1996): 46-84.

Sands, Roberta G., L. Alayne Parson, and Josann Duane. "Faculty Mentoring in a Public University." *The Journal of Higher Education* 62 (1991): 174-93.

Sorcinelli, Mary Deane. "Effective Approaches to New Faculty Development." *Journal of Counseling and Development* 72 (1994): 474-80.

St. Clair, Karen L. "Faculty to Faculty Mentoring in the Community College." *Community College Review* 22.3 (1994): 23-36.

Tierney, William G. "Organizational Socialization in Higher Education." *The Journal of Higher Education* 68 (1997): 1-16.

Zachary, Lois J. *The Mentor's Guide: Facilitating Effective Learning Relationships*. San Francisco: Jossey-Bass, 2000.

Part II

☙

Writing Group Two:
Looking Closely at Classroom Practices

Reading to Write; "Reading" the Classroom to Re-vise Learning

Sarah Robbins, Linda Stewart, and Renee Kaplan

The two essays that follow are linked both by our participation in a three-member writing group and by common themes that developed through discussions of our teaching as we shared our writing, in person and online. Our collaborative process was shaped by several factors, but especially by the fact that we were all three trying to write about teaching that was still very much in-process. While we were writing our essays, we were also in "draft mode" with our teaching: we were "reading" classroom practices that were still unfolding. That is, during the year when we were meeting to develop plans for the essays and (later) to compose our various drafts, we were still in the midst of the actual curriculum initiatives we were trying to document. Hence, our writing group shaped not only the essays' content but also the specific teaching experiences that are now recorded here. For instance, through our group collaboration, we all three gained a heightened awareness of the benefits associated with having students create written reflections about their learning processes, so we all began to allow more protected class time for this type of activity. In addition, we all read about and had our students use multi-genre forms for reporting on research. On that topic and others, we continually exchanged ideas about books and articles to read, as well as stories about what was going on in our classrooms. Looking back, we now find it difficult to identify which of us first came up with specific ideas that worked their way into the teaching and writing all three of us were sharing.

To work together, we did have to overcome some obstacles. At first, we had a fourth group member. Very early on, she decided that she was not ready to write about her topic for this publication, so our team shrank to three. Linda and Sarah were co-authoring an essay, so our group actually had only two pieces on which to collaborate, and that proved to be both beneficial and challenging. With only two essays in progress, we could read the pieces very closely. But we did lack the stimulation some of the larger groups had from reading more drafts all at once. (Trading drafts with members of other writing groups later on in the project did alleviate this problem, as we will outline below.)

Even after our group became smaller, we still faced logistical challenges. Our schedules never seemed compatible. In the initial stages, we couldn't seem to find a day that would work for all three of use to meet. Therefore, several times, we met in pairs rather than as a whole group of three. We would summarize these "pair-share" discussions via a whole-group email, so that all three of us could still stay informed. And soon we realized that the small size of our group could be advantageous: we could "meet online" simply by exchanging emailed drafts.

Indeed, after we had tried this approach, we discovered that it worked well for us. All three of us enjoy writing, and we were excited about our essays. Therefore, we didn't need to meet in person so frequently to keep our energy up. All of us enjoy reading about teaching, so we found it exciting every time a new revision appeared in our digital mailboxes, and we established a protocol of responding promptly to emailed drafts. Also, all of us are interested in technology-enhanced writing, so we were enthusiastic about experimenting with commenting and editing features of Word for Windows that might move our essays along. In the early drafting stages, we would write response notes directly into the word file we received online, putting queries in brackets and suggested changes in blue. Where we thought the text could be condensed, we used word's "strikeout" function. We also wrote longer, global responses at the end of draft files or in the email "box," including praise and questions.

Just as when we respond to student writing in written form, we found that our emailed notes on our colleagues' texts required us to think about giving feedback as a kind of art form in itself. We learned there is a fine balance between offering too much or too little help. We learned to ask good questions. We learned ways to help writers revise without heaping false praise or making caustic comments.

Below are excerpts from an online response sent to Renee—i.e., segments from one of Renee's very early drafts, with Sarah's and Linda's suggestions and questions in bold type, just as Renee would have seen it as a word attachment. (Sarah and Linda had synthesized their responses before emailing them, in this case.)

Sharing Journal Reflections of Inspiration and Remembrance
[We really like the title!]

"If you haven't attempted new avenues to incorporate technology into your lessons, now is the time to try," urged my middle school principal. **[great to open with a quote!]** I do believe that statement. Integrating technology with curriculum standards will bring harmony to my students' learning, and it will expand knowledge and skill development....

Being an experienced language arts teacher and a national Holocaust educator, I decided to develop a project to instruct my eighth grade ~~literacy class of~~ gifted students on how to integrate their knowledge of the Holocaust with first-person accounts of local survivors. ~~In short,~~ I envisioned that the students would interview survivors, listen to first-hand oral testimonies, digitally photograph and video these testimonies, and compose interview narratives. This **would** become a community-based project involving students, parents, local survivors, Apple Computer, Inc., the school's Partner in Education, and other professionals from universities and state and federal agencies. **[super background info in this paragraph!]**

The procedures of instruction prior to actual meetings and interviews with survivors involved a historical study of the Holocaust, excerpts of multi-genre literature, a literature study of a Holocaust memoir *All But My Life* by Gerda Weisssmann Klein, researching first person accounts of interviews on the internet websites at the United States Holocaust Memorial Museum, and viewing of Holocaust related videos. Journal writings were to be incorporated and shared throughout the lessons. The learning process involved **connecting** the **Georgia** State Standards **[for social studies? We're unclear about this link]** and the eighth grade language arts curriculum. **[Do you need to provide a "map" of your essay structure here—something like: In the sections of this essay that follow, to re-visit this teaching experience, I will present my own journal entries from the unit, along with representative samples from my students' reflections.]**

The finished essay has a different opening than that in the excerpt above, because, as Renee and her students worked together throughout the semester, their journaling gradually became more important than the technology focus with which she began. But some elements in her early draft remained in place through further revisions, and the suggestion to begin thinking about the essay's structure did encourage her to consider various organizational ideas—both for her essay and for the classroom project itself.

Once we saw how well our online responses to each other were working, Sarah and Linda did more of their collaborative writing by dividing up sections of their essay, working on them individually, and sending segments to each other by email, with each author commenting on the other's most recent drafting. Renee continued to email global questions about her text to Sarah and Linda, as well as sending whole drafts as attachments.

However, despite the role that online responding was playing in our group process, talking remained central to the group's writing. For Sarah's and Linda's co-authored essay, talking included extended discussions we had prior to revising our introduction and body based on making a new outline for our essay's structure. Having to articulate ideas about the piece's direction to each other at this stage clarified the narrative's argument and organizational agenda. Later, moving further into revision, talking was often the means for negotiating points of style—even individual word choice. Talking also highlighted gaps in our thinking or weaknesses in detail. Like our drafting, the revision process proceeded most smoothly when writing separately was complemented by personal discussions.

A highlight of our writing group process was a dinner to celebrate the completion of our first rough drafts. This occasion was actually the first time that Renee and Linda had met face-to-face. After that, our email exchanges and our cross-text editing became even more comfortable, detailed, and lively. But from the very beginning, an important trait of our collaboration was our willingness to be honest with each other and to accept constructive criticism as well as praise. For example, in a talk session early in the project, Renee tactfully rejected Sarah's tentative idea for an essay topic: Renee recommended that Sarah consider a classroom-oriented essay rather than writing about how to create ethnographies. Renee was urging Sarah to think about our anticipated cross-level readers and the interest they would have in teaching. Small though our group was, it embodied that cross-level audience—a fact which shaped our conversations, our writing, and the reading we continued throughout our revision stages.

Re-reading our essays now, we are not surprised to see some striking similarities in our classroom stories. Our conversations were shaping our teaching practices. For example, through discussing our drafts, we discovered that writing to learn in the eighth grade can be much like in a college classroom. Our essays also reflect a shared commitment to community-building and studying community life: in the projects described in both of our essays, students researched and wrote about the world outside their classroom, and the experience of "going public" strengthened the sense of community within our classrooms. In spite of the obvious differences between middle schools and universities, as we wrote together, our classrooms became more alike, linked by core concepts about collaborative, reflective writing that all of us were examining (and experimenting with) in our practice. The more we wrote, the more we saw the connecting points when we read each others' texts.

As we moved through multiple revisions, re-reading each others' work remained a crucial element in our group process, but expanding our reading base became important to our writing as well. Members of other writing groups in our community of practice recommended specific research pieces to us. As Renee has pointed out, having others in the project emphasize the importance of professional reading was significant in itself. In one reflective note she wrote: "It's really helpful to me to BE with people who read. Very few people in my school do. My principal does, and the one other NWP teacher in my building. But through this project, I am truly learning how to use research to support what I'm doing."

For all three of us, a major support to our writing process came from drafts that were being prepared in other writing groups linked to our community of practice. (See "Reading Across Writing Groups" in Part IV.) In reading Vicki Walker's essay, Sarah and Linda were able to recognize some core concepts driving their classroom decision-making. From reading Vicki's text, they were also encouraged to highlight the various *stages* their instructional program was using to shape their students' interactions with visual culture. In reading Deborah Kramb's essay, Renee saw points about professional growth that could be treated more explicitly in her own essay. Reading Deborah's essay also encouraged Renee to work harder on crafting a distinctive writing voice.

Reading the written response pieces we received from others in the inquiry community when they had reviewed our drafts was another key support to our revision. Vicki Walker (who was writing her own "Picture This" essay) read one of Sarah's and Linda's drafts. Vicki's questions prompted them to weave in more details about *how* their students were demonstrating their learning. Deborah Kramb read one of Renee's drafts. (See "Reading Across Writing Groups.") In Deborah's written response, we saw ways Renee could take fuller advantage of student voices in her text, providing additional analysis of their significance.

What advice would we give to other teachers who want to use writing groups to support their professional development? Our group's emphasis on online collaboration meant we were using different strategies than the other teacher-writers involved in this book's community of practice. But there were important commonalities with the other groups as well. One thing we learned is that it's worthwhile to talk about teaching, research, and writing practices as a step toward sharing with a wider audience. Talking to colleagues—and students—and documenting the ideas that emerge from these discussions are ways to begin writing. And it's essential to connect regularly with members of your group—to have a calendar for the work. Perhaps most of all, we learned that reading and writing can go hand in hand to promote professional development. Teachers who want to use writing to grow professionally should study examples of professional writing by teachers—both published pieces and in-process writing that colleagues are doing. Good writers read. Teachers' writing groups provide a powerful way to link reading and writing through collaborative reflection.

Sharing Journal Reflections of Inspiration and Remembrance in Holocaust Studies

Renee Kaplan
Mabry Middle School

My middle school rests in a suburban middle-class Atlanta community. Most students' parents are professionals, and they have high expectations for their children's achievement. Both students and parents value creativity, task completion, and intellectual growth. In the year when I joined the inquiry team for this project, one of my classes—an integrated literacy course—was composed of twenty-one gifted eighth grade students. We met once every day for forty-eight minutes. These students had already attained scores in the 97th percentile and above on standardized tests in Reading and Language. They were ready for a learning challenge.

Being a nationally trained Holocaust educator, I decided to develop a project to instruct my gifted students on how to enhance basic knowledge of the Holocaust with first-person accounts of local survivors. (See Totten.) This essay revisits the learning processes through which these students and I used an inquiry-based journaling approach to respond to their study of the Holocaust.

My eighth grade students have always done expressive writing assignments. I encourage students to think about their learning experiences and record responses in a reflection log or journal. Before this project, I had always wanted to share my own journal writing and my studies of the Holocaust with students as a means of encouragement and connection to their learning. After all, Moffett advises that collaborative inquiry is active learning: "Witnessing, attuning, imitating, helping, collaborating, and interacting occur so spontaneously, just as part of living, that we seldom think of these six basic learning activities as education. . . . Investigating makes use of all means, from witnessing and experimenting to interviewing other people and researching the symbolized information transmitted from the past" (161).

Several questions guided this classroom project. First, I asked, how can my students and I use journaling to discover our written voices and share attitudes, opinions, and emotions about our learning process? Second, I wondered how first-hand testimonies by Holocaust survivors could enrich knowledge and student engagement with this challenging topic. Also I questioned whether using collaborative reflective writing in the classroom might help us process the challenging material at the heart of Holocaust studies in a productive way. Reflective writing in journals, we found, was especially productive for our study of the Holocaust—a topic that is personally moving, emotionally intense, and intellectually challenging.

My initial concept for this project came to me after I viewed the iPhoto program at an Apple Computer Store. Originally, I envisioned that the students would interview survivors, listen to first-hand oral testimonies, digitally photograph and video these testimonies, and then publish multimedia-based interview narratives. Their work, I hoped, would be a community-based project involving students, parents, local survivors, and Apple Computer, Inc., the school's Partner in Education. The end product I imagined seemed an especially good way to meet a call from our principal to "incorporate technology into your lessons." However, along the way, the process of doing the research and reflecting on it gradually extended itself to the point where this class did not achieve my original goal for a final publication. But their learning was important and powerful, nonetheless, and it centered in our shared processes of inquiry and reflection.

Just as I was beginning this project, colleagues at the Kennesaw Mountain Writing Project were starting to collaborate on a study of reflection and writing by teachers investigating their own practices for professional development. Meanwhile, I was seeking advice from some of those same colleagues about the unit I was preparing to teach. I decided to join one of that team's writing groups. Thus, written reflection journals began to develop for my students and me at the same time, and I really began to feel like a mentor to the students in a new way. I had never actually shared journal writing with students before. I had read along with them, but had never written alongside them, other than to comment on and grade their compositions. This project led me to become a writer *with* my students. Therefore, drawing on collaboration with my teacher writing group and my students, this essay provides a record of shared reflection and writing-to-learn.

Oral histories focus on people, not statistics. So the first step in conducting an oral history project is to select a subject that is of high interest and historical importance, like the Holocaust. Learning how to conduct interviews was a new goal for my students, and so we needed to spend time researching effective interview techniques. Together, the students and I developed questions appropriate for each survivor we interviewed and then synthesized our knowledge together. This collaborative work built on research by David Lindquist, who has pointed out that in Holocaust studies, "Students [can] become so immersed in the event that they begin to think in sophisticated ways, often raising the overall level of their academic activities" (66).

Meetings and interviews with survivors needed to be prefaced, however, with a historical study of the Holocaust. Our class used examples of multi-genre literature; a Holocaust memoir, *All But My Life*, by Gerda Weisssmann Klein; accounts of interviews on the internet websites of the United States Holocaust Memorial Museum; and Holocaust-related videos. The entire project extended over a three-month period from February through April. We used journal writings throughout the study, aiming to generate and document a learning process connecting Georgia's standards for teaching research skills with the eighth grade language arts curriculum. To retrace my teaching experience, and to suggest how the collaborative writing with my students helped me manage a challenging teaching experience, the remainder of this essay will revisit excerpts from our journals and set them within a narrative of the project's history. While acquiring important knowledge about the Holocaust, we learned additional lessons about writing to learn, especially when that writing is done in a social context. (See Young and the closing chapter of this book, "Teachers' Writing Groups in Context.")

Journal Reflections Shaping Curriculum
Teacher's Reflection - January 30, 2003

How do I begin? What am I thinking? How can I pull this off in three or four months? When will I teach other language arts classes and grade papers? Uh oh, I am overwhelmed already! My juices are flowing; I am energized and excited. I need permission slips for off-campus travel. I need legal copyright forms for the survivors, and for the use of photos I scan or insert from other resources. Let's face it; I need lots of help. Let the process begin; I will stumble, I may even fall, I will get up, then put on a Band-Aid, and continue.

I first discussed all of my ideas with my principal, Dr. Tim Tyson. He was very supportive and immediately contacted our representative from our school's partner in education, Apple Computer, Inc. The Apple Computer representative told Dr. Tyson that the project appeared to be just what Apple was looking for, to show actual student technology use and learning through integrated curriculum. Dr. Tyson then asked me to write a prospectus for the project. Since I had never written one, I became flustered. But I took the proposals I had done for presentations at professional conferences, a genre which I have written before, and proceeded from there. I shared the prospectus with my principal, and he submitted it to Apple.

I knew I needed to engage student learning and promote personal growth. Some questions emerged about the instructional process:

- How could I design creative journal prompts to help students meaningfully reflect on their learning?
- What would be the best progression of activities to use for this project?
- How could I assess the acquisition and use of knowledge about the Holocaust?

Teacher's Reflection - February 3, 2003

Filled with excitement, I introduce this project to the students. All of the students know of my involvement in Holocaust education and that the study of the Holocaust is a part of the eighth grade curriculum. I anticipate positive comments from the students regarding their desire to study the Holocaust, interview survivors, and produce a book composed of photographs and survivor testimonies.

Students responded honestly to their feelings about studying the Holocaust and interviewing survivors. Several young men showed reluctance in their reflections, and I initially had trouble understanding their perspective.

Students' Reflections - February 3, 2003

Daniel: *"I do not want to do this project. I do not really understand it."*

Michael: *"I feel this is not of my interest, and I would like to be in another Literacy class."*

While I was initially discouraged by some of the reactions, others were more positive:

Melissa: *"This project sounds pretty cool. I'm not psyched beyond words because it sounds like a huge undertaking, but it sounds very interesting."*

Alyssa: *"The first time my teacher, Mrs. Kaplan, told me about the iPhoto project we are going to do, I was thinking, 'Oh Joy! Another boring learning project.' Then, the more I heard about the project, the more I liked it. It sounded more fun and different than the usual projects that I have done for other classes."*

I decided to share the students' reactions with the principal; together we agreed to include those reluctant students and proceed with the project as planned. I wanted to engage them despite their initial resistance. The principal and I together decided they would be responsible for the Holocaust history, the readings and writing in the class, but not the actual interviews, if they did not want to participate. I pledged to express my respect for their honesty in private, individual conversations with the students and their parents via phone calls and emails. The two young men who had been reluctant decided that this could become a great project, but they still felt some shyness and fear.

With the range of my students' journal reflections in mind, we next focused on writing a rationale for studying the Holocaust so as to clarify our goals and objectives. We planned to revisit the rationale statements again near the end of the project. The statements would become a means of evaluating the students' understanding about studying the Holocaust and the application of knowledge learned from the survivors. Student draft rationale statements ranged widely from vague understanding to no concept of the content whatsoever. But many students did appear to be making a connection between the unit's goals and related vocabulary words we had discussed, such as "prejudice and hatred" and "genocide."

Students' Reflections - February 4, 2003

Alyssa: *"I am very indecisive and cannot answer that question about rationale at this time."*

Grant: *"To prevent genocides and extreme acts of hatred from ever happening again through educating our generation about the horrors of the Holocaust."*

Erin: *"I think people study the Holocaust so they are better informed about the past, and people teach it so younger generations don't make the same mistakes of the past."*

Teacher's Reflection - February 10, 2003

At this point in the process, the pedagogical details are becoming overwhelming; I need to pick the brains of the experts. . . . Sylvia Wygoda, Chairperson of the Georgia Commission on the Holocaust, and Stephen Feinberg, Director of National Outreach in the Education Division of the United States Holocaust Memorial Museum…offered helpful suggestions. We discussed ideas such as motivating students, obtaining addresses and phone numbers of local survivors, setting up appointments for interviews, posing appropriate interview questions, bringing survivors to [my school] for oral testimonies, arranging the visual layouts of pages in the book, and using pictures and maps from published materials and the internet for the class publication.

Teacher's Reflection - March 6, 2003

Students need to have time for reflection on their learning, whether reading a selection, discussing in groups, note taking from teacher's lectures. . . . Response writing may work best immediately after the learning experience. I, as well as almost all the teachers I know, do not make the time nor have the time to devote to this activity in class. In language arts, this should probably be the closing activity..., not an initial class activity. Let students think and write about what they did or did not learn or feel during a lesson.

How to attract students for writing to learn is sometimes a problem. Does one student do the reflective writing just because it is assigned while another is ready to leap into the process? How about this free writing method? Should it only be prose or can it be sketches or even in poetic format? Length is also a [question]. Can one express a thought as a metaphor or simile while another needs to describe a feeling in a full page? Rather than elaboration, my eighth grade students want to find the shortest route to achieve the assignment.

They always ask: "How long does this have to be? Do I need a full page? Can I skip lines? Do I need a title? How come she writes so much, and I can say what I want to say in a few lines? Do I need five sentences per paragraph?"

Re-reading my journal now, I see how hard I was working to think about writing and to avoid being discouraged that all my students were not enthusiastic about the topic.

[My] students...are not as excited as I had anticipated for them to be. They have finished reading All But My Life; I now need to try different strategies to motivate those who are blasé about this project.... Am I over estimating [my students'] abilities as eighth graders?... Will the students really be able to accomplish all of this in a short time? How many interviews can we actually do?... I feel overwhelmed, and that this project is growing like the Southern vine, kudzu. It is taking over my life.... I feel tangled and my method of instruction for the written reflection is a weave or braid rather than a straight direction of thoughts and feelings. I am the type of teacher who needs constant mental stimulation, so I go home and think and read about ways to incorporate multi-genre writing, Holocaust survivors' interviews, oral history projects, pedagogy on reflective and responsive writing, and the latest research on technology integration?... What is my reasoning behind all of this?... I am now wondering: is reflective writing becoming a tool to my understanding of the process of written instruction. Do I reflect, write, and teach? Or do I teach, reflect, and write? How will this change as I really delve deeply into my own thoughts and feelings about student learning and the process of writing for self-expression? I am now imagining a circular order of reflection <–> writing <–> teaching, and I am beginning to learn that no one single method comes first before the other.

Looking back at these journal entries, I can see that I was tapping more and more deeply into the power of writing to learn. As a teacher, I realize I am writing all the time, just as I am reading all the time. I write vast multi-genre materials: lessons; emails; notes to students, parents, and colleagues; proposals, and more. But I now know, reading back over my journal, that all my writing does not have to be in these professional formats; some of it should be truly exploratory. Reflective writing makes a difference for me because my written voice is different than my spoken voice. I feel that my written voice is an echo of genuine feelings and thoughts. My spoken voice is the one I usually use in the classroom. It feels the push and hurry of addressing multiple demands for curriculum delivery. I now feel that my written voice is a truer echo of feelings and thoughts as a teacher. Once I let my writing voice into the classroom, I slowed down and reflected on learning with my students. (See Fletcher.)

Students' Reflections - March 10, 2003

Students wrote approximately twice a week in journals. One prompt midway through the project asked the students to think about how they felt about interviewing survivors.

Daniel (one of the students who was resistant at first): *"I will feel more motivated when we get into the interviewing part of the project. [But] I would be scared that the survivors might be embarrassed or insulted by our questions."*

Michael (another of the initially reluctant students): *"I feel the cause, knowing what this project is for, has made me more motivated. This is an important subject and this project should show it. I want this project to be great. The victims could be sad and cry about telling us their story. This would make it very sad."*

Melissa: *"Interviewing survivors will be scary, sensitive, and uncertain because they have gone through many tragic events that will be hard for us to 'stomach'."*

Jackie: *"The area of this project that will make me feel more motivated is the actual interaction with the survivors. I feel that just seeing the people who lived through such a time will be inspiring. A project of interviewing survivors is very informative and almost in some aspects scary. ... [I]n my sheltered life; I have never encountered any real hardships myself."*

Seeing the students' blend of excitement and apprehension in these entries, we were able to work through these feelings in open discussion of this writing, becoming prepared for the interviews even as we noted the complexity of doing primary research on the Holocaust.

Teacher's Reflection - March 19, 2003

I have never really realized sharing written reflections with my students could promote such in-depth relationship of learning experiences; I feel like a mentor to students, acquiring knowledge with them. When I read my journal entries to them, they applaud, and I feel embarrassed because that is not my reason for sharing. The atmosphere becomes extremely personal; sharing gives me an opportunity to explore my teaching styles and reflect upon the richness of instructing and collaborating with students. Experimenting [with] collaborative reflective writing [shows me] that I must be a learner from my students.

Teacher's Reflection - March 24, 2003

I now feel . . . that the students are sophisticated enough to comprehend the information from the interviews and the emotions they feel as well. The heart and soul of this project is the creativity and the collaboration of young middle school students with senior adults in the community. Maybe these senior individuals and the students can become living examples of what education should be....Each story should chronologically tell about a time in history that is unique; it puts key events in context by looking back in time as well as looking forward....Deciding upon the way to retell the interview will be a monumental and frustrating task. Students will [need to] paraphrase some information that survivors mentioned as well as add personal movements, such as a tearful eye or a nod. Interpreting accents is also difficult.

All the time, I wake up thinking about this project of interviewing Holocaust survivors. I think of the challenging concepts we are discovering together....When students have interaction with each other and the survivors, and voice opinions in their speaking and writing, they feel a sense of ownership of their learning.

Teacher's Reflection - March 26, 2003

I had the privilege to speak to three survivors [Stephen Feinberg, Bert Lewyn, and Eugen Schoenfeld] *on the telephone today. One I will visit tomorrow, and the two others I have arranged for class visits. Listening to a survivor speak stays with me. I need to create a classroom atmosphere that is comfortable for the survivor and the students. Survivors may speak of their lives before the war, of the personal losses they experienced, of their days in concentration camps, and of liberation and coming to America. A glimpse is all we ask for.*

A big issue is to be respectful and sensitive to the victims of the Holocaust. Elie Wiesel explains, "The Holocaust is not a subject like all the others. It imposes certain limits....In order not to betray the dead and humiliate the living, this particular subject demands a special sensibility, a different approach, a rigor, strengthened by respect and reverence and, above all, faithfulness to memoir" (167-168).

Students viewed Courage To Care, a video profiling rescuers, non-Jews who risked their lives to protect Jews from Nazi persecution. Students wrote responses afterwards. Several expressed admiration for the rescuers.

Students' Reflections – April 1, 2003

Michael: *"It is great knowing how much these people care, knowing that they put their lives on the line to save other peoples' lives. They have great pride and huge hearts to do such acts of unselfishness."*

Ann: *"It takes a lot of guts to risk your life for someone else. It must have been scary to know you could be killed at one certain moment for risking your own life for another. If more had done this during the Holocaust, maybe not so many people would have been killed."*

Two survivors came on different days and shared their oral testimonies with the students. One man lived in Berlin, Germany, during WWII and was a Jewish victim on the run, or "U-boater." The other, son of a survivor, was a toddler during the war, hidden in Romania. After these visits, I offered two open-ended questions for journaling: "What have you found beneficial about hearing the first two survivors' testimonies?" and "What was the most important message you learned from the survivors?" (See Totten.)

Students' Reflections - April 16, 2003

John: *"I think it is beneficial hearing from actual survivors because there is less room for error in a first-hand account as opposed to a misinterpretation in a second-hand account. Who knows better the actual pain and fear than one who experienced it? I also learned details that a textbook would never portray."*

Jessi: *"Their two different stories showed different perspectives in their involvements in the Holocaust. They showed that no one has the same Holocaust experience. Every story is different....One survivor mentioned something that meant a lot to me. He said, 'We are all different on the outside, but on the inside we are all the same.' By saying that, I think he meant that people should look past their appearances or races because everyone wants to be accepted, meaning that we are all alike."*

Jamie: *"I was able to picture the places and things that were happening as they were telling their story. It made me think more about the people it was affecting than just hearing it from the teacher. The facial expressions and voices of the two men seemed to make it real, and made me realize it was a very tragic event that happened not so long ago."*

Matt: *"It was better than just reading about it from a book because the information was coming from first hand experiences. It also showed how survivors came to America and can become successful after going through the Holocaust. They made new lives for themselves."*

Chelsea responds: *"I found out how important it is to listen to others' experiences. And it made me realize how lucky I am to live in America and be as safe and free as I am."*

Allison: *"This showed how in the midst of uncertainty and fear, one can still have hope.... One even got a chance to play professional basketball as a Jewish immigrant. I really enjoyed how he shared his story and tried to truly convey the message that the Holocaust really did happen."*

A week later, with the end the time available for the project fast approaching, I gave the students another prompt designed to help them think through how their own work of recording the interviews would become an archive for next years' students to draw upon to complete the Holocaust memory book. Our prompt was: How do you feel about doing the process of the interviews and thinking about students working next year to prepare a publication?

Students' Reflections - April 23, 2003

Alyssa: *"I think that this is fine because then you can see more points of view and that develops a better understanding of what the Holocaust was like. And since different people will be in the class next year, that just means that more will learn about the Holocaust."*

Greg: *"I feel disappointed that we can't continue the project because I was interested in interviewing more Holocaust survivors and hearing their stories. I also wanted the satisfaction of having helped make the iPhoto Book. Then another small part of me feels excited for the next group of students who get to work on this project."*

Daniel: *"I feel sort of frustrated that I can't finish something I started. It is really suspenseful, kind of like when a good movie abruptly ends, and I have to wait until the sequel. I really anticipate finishing this project."*

Amonae: *"I feel kind of disappointed because I wanted to see the finished product, but at the same time I am proud that the project got so big that we can't even finish it.... Everyone had heard of it and was talking about it."*

Students were also asked to revisit our earlier questions about a rationale for studying the Holocaust today.

Daniel: *"It's simple; we want people to be informed especially kids, so in the future people will remember what happened and hopefully history won't repeat itself."*

Paul: *"I think now that the rationale for studying the Holocaust is because it was an act of pure evil that was committed only a few decades ago by educated* *people against society. It should not be repeated, and the only way to prevent it is to teach younger generations the truth of it. We should appreciate human rights."*

Erin: *"'I [would] teach the subject because the world is full of hate and history can repeat itself,' said Mr. Kessler, a survivor. I agree with this. We study the subject to educate today's youth so a new Hitler won't arise. We also study because it happened quite recently and in an important time in history. It also occurred throughout Europe, a cultured and educated location in the world during the 20th century. Our rationale is to educate young people and to teach them individual responsibility and what to do with their lives."*

Looking Back and Forward

David Lindquist has observed that "teaching and studying the Holocaust becomes a profoundly moving experience for educators and students" (203). By putting together faces of real people with facts and stories, survivors bring the subject to life for students. All the details survivors report are part of an immense picture; every family, every place, every friend, every job was erased, and trying to rebuild each survivor's memory supports an interplay between history, morality, and human spirit. The current personalities of the survivors are layers of private experiences that no one can fully comprehend. But sharing living history with today's youth is the most real educational experience I can think of. This class project promoted the collection of memories of the human spirit. I hope the finished Holocaust memory book will become a keepsake, a provoker of memories, a guide to relationships between children and seniors in the community.

Like the collaborative research for this classroom project, learning to write reflectively is a process. It becomes easier if it is shared with others in the learning stages. My beliefs about writing have changed because of the sharing of honest reflections with my students. Of special importance to me as a teacher is the fact that I will continue to use this approach in the future.

How do I know this collaborative, reflective method of teaching about the Holocaust was effective? For one thing, we did evaluations of learning through writing tied to our initial goals and rationale. When reading students' journals, I used the following "positive feature" rubric for formative assessment, based on traits of effective reflective writing shared with the class:

- "The journal entry is concise and easy to follow."
- "The journal entry focuses on personal thoughts and feelings about the topic or experience."

- "The journal entry expresses a clear opinion, along with supporting reasons."
- "The journal entry shows the personal meaning or value of the topic for the learner."
- "The journal entry shows the writer is willing to take risks and attempt new ideas."

Did students write profound journal response statements? Some did, more than others, but they all expressed honest opinions, fears, and hopes through interaction with peers, survivors, and me. For example, some indicated that may never again be as innocent, as secure, or as naive in their feelings that good triumphs over evil—but that confronting these themes was important for personal growth. And, at the same time, I could see in their journal entries how students increasingly emphasized themes of personal responsibility and ethics.

Students did write to learn. They expressed honest thoughts; they shared feelings and beliefs; they also gained a valuable understanding of a learning process as tentative, since the end product publication would not be finished until later, by another group. They learned that producing a quality, "finished" product takes time and becomes a journey that should be enjoyed as we travel to the destination.

Reflection

This was my first experience writing about my classroom for publication. I learned a number of basic skills for professional writing. For instance, this was actually the first time I had done revisions and editing using technology—the software in Word for Windows that supports these stages of writing. I also learned about formatting and citing. Exchanging our drafts online taught me a new approach to editing.

Working with my small writing group and the larger inquiry team also brought new thinking to my classroom, because I was writing about an instructional project that was still very much in process. Answering questions from readers in the project pushed me to critique my teaching. By joining a community of teacher writers, I became able to explain my new instructional project to my students more effectively. Significantly, while I was gaining suggestions for improvement from colleagues in my writing group, I was also learning to work along with my students differently than in the past. Through shared journaling, my students and I became co-researchers trying out a new approach for studying the Holocaust. Our shared reflective writing monitored and guided the flow of the instructional unit and eventually led to the focus of this essay.

Initially, even when I was journaling along with students in my classroom, I found that my primary audience was myself. In the next stages, my writing group became my main audience, as I was gradually transforming journal entries and combining them with new analysis. At that point, my writing became part of a collaborative writing group's process, and finally it took shape into an essay for professional publication. Along the way, I learned how to describe, analyze, and reflect on varieties of journaling that were going on in my class. Gaining more practice in writing to analyze my teaching helped give me confidence to do more professional writing.

Using writing and then reflecting on my writing, I discovered that I was willing to take risks as the Holocaust project developed. It became much larger in scope than I originally planned. As the power of journaling in my classroom grew, the students became enthusiastic about shared writing experiences and about their research into the Holocaust. They really enjoyed listening to my written reflections, and I saw how modeling writing to learn was encouraging them to write in new, more exploratory ways in their own journals. Now, with the groups of students I've had since the project described here, I still share my writing.

Moving from using my journal writing to improve my own classroom instruction to writing about shared journal writing for an audience beyond my classroom was a challenging step for me, however. I had trouble deciding how to organize my material at first. My group helped me by asking questions until I recognized the right approach to take; their feedback wasn't a telling—it was a questioning—and then I identified a plan through my own cognitive process, through questioning and dialogue. For example, I had difficulty deciding upon the organization of my reflections and the students' reflections. My writing group encouraged me to start by revisiting my reflections about the project in chronological order. This step led me to recognize how my management of the classroom journaling had changed over time. Gradually, I had developed more meaningful writing prompts for students that would show their knowledge and feelings—to me and to each other. Reviewing my own and my students' journal entries also led me to see that sharing the reflective writing process with my students had made the learning environment caring, individualized, respectful, and challenging for everyone. Then I realized that my essay should be a chronological narrative, taking the reader along on our classroom journey, moving back and forth between my journal and my students' reflective writing.

Through journaling, the students also changed as learners. In the beginning, some were reluctant about studying and writing about the Holocaust. As my writing team pointed out to me, the project was very large in scope and therefore challenging for eighth graders to comprehend as a "whole" piece of learning, one blending writing, historical research, oral history, and technology. Some students became frightened, and a few did not want to participate. Through discussions and written reflections, their reluctance, along with the age-appropriate feelings behind it, became apparent. Some were especially afraid of meeting strangers, in this case the survivors who had experienced the Holocaust. At the same time, sharing their journal entries showed that many were excited about the project, and hearing that enthusiasm in writing encouraged others. I was sharing my journal too, of course. As my students listened to my thoughts about the project and how I praised their responses, my classroom became a community. They started to assume ownership of the project and spoke of feeling special because it was unique. Students' writing improved due to the extra practice, the sharing of ideas, and their feelings of project ownership.

All along the way, I invited my students to use the practices that I was learning through work with my own small writing group. Oral sharing became a major part of our classroom. Students shared responses in pairs and in small groups; some volunteered to share with the whole class. Often they literally applauded their peers and encouraged extended discussion of each other's entries, leading us to deep insights. Reading, thinking, speaking, listening, and writing became entwined, as journaling became a productive routine for promoting learning.

Based on the experiences of being a part of a small writing group, a community of practice, and a community of writers in the classroom, I now recognize the importance of collaboration. Teachers need motivation as much as students do. Successful teams respect each other's ideas and value suggestions for improvement. Discussing pedagogy and sharing best practices with my teacher colleagues promote leadership which extends into the classroom. We develop as writers and grow as learners. One way this happened in my classroom during this project was that I shared our writing group's reflections-on-process with my students. That helped them value the writing process; it made collaboration seem real. Now, in my classroom, we don't know the outcome when we begin a learning enterprise. We get there together.

References

The Courage to Care. Dir. Robert A. Gardner. Anti-Defamation League, 1986.

Feinberg, Stephen. Personal interview. 31 Jan. 2003.

Fletcher, Ralph. *What a Writer Needs*. Portsmouth: Heinemann, 1993.

Kessler, Andre. Personal interview. 15 April 2003.

Klein, Gerda Weissmann. *All But My Life*. New York: Hill and Wang, 1996.

Lewyn, Bert. Personal interview. 3 April 2003.

Lindquist, David Hays. *Toward Pedagogy of the Holocaust: Perspectives of Exemplary Teachers*. Bloomington: Indiana UP, 2002.

Moffett, James. *The Universal Schoolhouse: Spiritual Awakening Through Education*. Portland: Calendar Islands Publishers, 1998.

Schoenfeld, Gene. Personal interview. 27 March 2003.

Totten, Samuel. "Incorporating First-Person Accounts into a Study of the Holocaust." *Teaching and Studying the Holocaust*. Ed. Samuel Totten and Stephen Feinberg. Boston: Allyn and Bacon, 2001. 107-38.

Tyson, Tim. Personal interview. 30 Jan. 2003.

Wiesel, Elie. *From the Kingdom of Memory: Reminiscences*. New York: Summit Books, 1990.

Wygoda, Sylvia. Personal interview. 31 Jan. 2003.

Young, Art. *Teaching Writing Across the Curriculum*. 3rd ed. Upper Saddle River: Prentice Hall, 1999.

"Seeing" Community: Visual Culture in College Composition

Sarah Robbins and Linda Stewart
Kennesaw State University

For the past several years, as participants on a grant-funded teacher inquiry team, the two of us have been researching Northwest Georgia's regional culture and its connections with the formation of American community life. (See the Keeping and Creating American Communities website at http://kcac.kennesaw.edu). At the same time, we've been experimenting with approaches for introducing general education students to community studies approaches similar to those we've been using ourselves. This essay concentrates on experiences from one semester when we were teaching separate sections of freshman composition but meeting frequently to share ideas and experiences.

We work at Kennesaw State University, located about 25 miles north of downtown Atlanta and perched just beside the interstate highway that carries thousands of commuters from suburban homes to jobs in the city, then back again at night. Over the past decade, as the daily traffic along I-75 has become more and more congested, a host of other changes has marked the areas around the university. Farms have given way to subdivisions, and longtime suburban communities have seen their shrinking green spaces filled with shopping malls and apartment complexes. Conflicts rooted in the changes going on in our region are always in the forefront of students' daily lives, so we have also placed these tensions at the heart of our curriculum, by inviting our classes to research the communities where they live.

One especially productive strategy emerging from this research has been to focus on visual culture. Accordingly, this essay will situate our developing goals for encouraging students to see the places they live within a larger context of community studies. We will also describe techniques we're using to build visual culture into student writing, and we will outline some of the ways these experiences are shaping our own teaching.

What is the Role of "Visual Culture" in Community Studies?

Collaborating with our students throughout the term, we investigate communities which are not merely geographic, but are also social groups and sites shaped by shared languages, beliefs, value systems, rituals and activities. (See "Curricular Program," KCAC website.) We study communities by asking where they are (in both real and virtual spaces) and how they do cultural work. Practically speaking, we are exploring the local landscapes where our students live their daily lives. These landscapes—whether the overcrowded parking lots on campus or the interactive space linking the local living room with scenes on CNN—are all marked by visual evidence of communities-in-formation. Thus, the content of our research and our writing includes the multi-faceted visual texts around us—in malls, homes, and town squares; in newsletters, bulletin boards, and web sites; on subdivision signs, sculptures, graffiti, and yard art; through town meetings, protests, and parades.

Our work with visual texts in community studies rests on recent scholarship exploring the cultural power of social images. Richard Howells, for example, suggests that we and our students need "to pay remedial attention" to "visual communication today." In particular, he asserts: "If we are unable to read visual culture, we are at the mercy of those who write it on our behalf" (5, 4). Thus, we try to support our students' moves to understand visual elements in the culture all around them and, when appropriate, to resist (or at least to question) those messages. Along those lines, in an end-of-course reflection, one of our students described the process that moved her from careful reading of a discount store's advertisement for the Barbie "happy family" toys to an inquiry into how suburban families are represented, represent themselves, and are reproduced in material culture objects.

Although we encourage our students to think conceptually, we try to avoid overwhelming them with theory for its own sake. Instead of having our students read highly theoretical essays, we create instructional activities encouraging them to interpret and create rhetorically sophisticated visual texts themselves. For instance, we wanted to address a topic like the role of photography as a meaning-making process. As preparation, the two of us read John Tagg's theoretical analysis of photography as evidence that "rests not on a natural or existential fact, but on a social, semiotic process"—part of a "complex historical outcome" generating meaning "only with certain institutional practices and within particular historical relations" (qtd. in Jay 270). Then, to make such concepts accessible to our students, we presented Tagg's basic ideas in relation to actual visual images gathered from around our own communities. In other words, from our students' perspective, we study visual culture in an experiential context. While as instructors we ground our teaching in theory, our students usually move to concepts about visual culture more inductively.

A truism of composition teaching at the college level (or at any level) is that good readers make good writers. So, when we took on the goal of teaching students to integrate effective visual elements into their writing, we knew we would also need to enhance their ability to read the visual environment. Below are two examples of the kinds of images we have used as a springboard for discussing community life and visual culture to prepare students for both kinds of intellectual work—reading and writing the visual—in their own compositions.

Introducing Students to Key Concepts and Practices: Using Video Clips in Class Discussion

As a starting point for visual culture analysis linked to community studies, we have found two approaches using film to be effective. First, we use discussion of the basic narrative content of individual films to introduce students to some themes and research questions associated with studies of community life. Along those lines, we have presented thematically similar segments from *The Simpsons, Sunshine State*, and *American Beauty*. Each of these video texts includes striking scenes about real estate's place in American life: for example, Marge's moral dilemma about becoming a realtor, the tensions between local Florida beachfront homeowners and out-of-state developers, and the Annette Benning character's various sales pitches to her diverse potential homebuyers. Particularly when we discuss them together in class, these films illuminate the complexities of the suburban landscape and the dynamic nature of community formation. By interpreting particular visual images together, students begin to understand that suburbia (like all community life) is *constructed*, as Kenneth Jackson suggests, "[as] a planning type and a state of mind based on imagery and symbolism" (4-5). Through guided class discussion, visual images in the films interact with students' own experience of place to prompt their exploration of communities, encouraging all of us to look closer at our particular neighborhoods, the larger community, and the artful representations of these spaces.

Our second approach involves more explicit consideration of specific visual images from film as a vehicle for representing and interpreting particular community issues. For example, on one occasion, we paired John Cusack's well-known dinner table riff in *Say Anything* (where he describes how he doesn't want to "manufacture anything processed, or process anything manufactured") with *The Graduate's* opening scenes. Elements in the staging of the Cusack scene that students notice include the interaction at the dinner table (a variation on positive stereotypes of suburban family meals), the other characters' puzzled facial expressions in response to Cusack's brutally honest comments, and the image of the family's father abruptly leaving the table. When we juxtapose that scene's use of the family home landscape with Mike Nichols' 1960s' depiction of California suburban parents celebrating their son's graduation, our students "see" how visual imagery can literally "make visible" complex arguments about community life, and how naming such themes can authenticate our otherwise-inchoate ideas about where and how we live.

Using Material Culture Objects as a Focus for Discussion

Reading images in video clips helps prepare our students for their primary research on daily life in America. Acting as visual anthropologists, in a sense, the students begin to actively explore our region of northwest Georgia, especially the changing rural, suburban, and ex-urban areas around Kennesaw State. To encourage students to look carefully and closely, we often invite them to examine objects of material culture. If they choose to visit a historical site or a model home, for example, we ask them to pick up a brochure. If they're flipping through the newspaper, we prompt them to note the advertisements. In conjunction with observing material culture, we ask them to question how these products represent the history of a site, the communities of a city, or the mission of a corporation. To encourage this interrogation of the representational nature of material culture, we have introduced familiar objects into the classroom for critical analysis.

For instance, we've found that the ubiquitous Starbucks coffee cup illustrates the layers of meaning in material culture. Details we've noted include the graphic mermaid-queen encircled in green and white. "Starbuck's Coffee" is named three times on one side of the cup. The green logo repeats the franchise name in a bolder, block font. Below the logo, the website <starbucks.com> appears. In italics: *Grande*. In class discussion, students have noted the company has its own language. These observations yield conversations about corporate image, marketing, and culture. For the servers' convenience, check boxes on the side are labeled with 'decaf', 'shots', 'syrup', 'milk', 'custom', and 'drink.' But other language is clearly aimed at the consumer: "There is a hidden magic in Starbucks coffee; proper brewing releases the subtle bouquet of flavors stored in each bean." These words float over the repeated tagline "We Proudly Brew Starbucks Coffee." Last, we observe the warning "Careful! The beverage you are about to enjoy is extremely hot!" The advertising mantra, the company statement, the logo, and the plea (framed to avoid lawsuits) suggest the multiple forces that combined to create the interrelated images on this paper cup. Clearly, as our students have come to "see" through examination of this single material object, coffee is a complicated business in modern suburbia.

From this seemingly simple activity, students begin to understand that observing their community involves not only looking carefully at images that surround them, but also questioning how material culture can lull us into internalizing certain cultural values that we should in fact interrogate. An exercise like this one can serve as one step in leading students to investigate their local region's visual landscape. Along those lines, during an online class discussion, Laila, one of Linda's students, pointed to messages embedded in the Atlanta skyline: "We are in constant motion to change because staying the same means we are falling behind somehow. Everything has to be bigger and better than it was before. One example… is the building of skyscrapers. There is always a challenge to build a taller building."

Students Writing About Their Reading of Visual Culture

Once students have gotten comfortable analyzing visual culture texts collaboratively through class discussion, we move to the next step: asking them to write about their own interpretations. One of our most generative assignments has been the site visit. This research assignment asks students to begin to understand the complex nature of their communities by selecting, visiting, and observing a location of their choice. The purpose of this activity is to further their understanding of the power of place and access to space through images of their region—in our case, metro Atlanta. While this assignment reinforces the concept of looking closely—whether the "text" is a neighborhood creek, a laboratory, a soccer field, a manufacturing plant, or an historical landmark—it also makes students aware that they are immersed in images that shape their perceptions.

Lucy Lippard, when discussing the artist's role in social experience in *The Lure of the Local*, states, "To affect perception itself, we need to apply ideas as well as forms to the ways in which people see and act within and on their surroundings" (286). By way of their site observation, framed through the lens of community studies, students begin to deepen their perceptions, understanding the complex nature of communities, how these communities create images, and how those images ultimately tell stories. Students have analyzed familiar surroundings with fresh eyes. They learn to critique the family history written on the walls of their homes, the competing agendas of mountain bikers and dog walkers, the social classes at their local discount store, and the clustering of groups on the high school bleachers during a football game. Others explore sites previously unfamiliar to them: garage sales, a barn preserved by the historic society, or a truck stop. Students observe how these sites often reveal, preserve, or transmit embedded values within contemporary culture. The resulting compositions, combining on-site observation with academic inquiry, often result in student writing that is engaged, interactive, and perceptive.

As students' eyes become attuned to reading their visual landscape, student writing has been transformed. Their critical thinking, their research, and their audiences have changed in three ways. First, students' perceptions are deepened. Their reflections often state how they now see their landscape differently, thinking about manipulation by marketing images, questioning the gating of their subdivisions, or noticing diminishing farmland and the spread of asphalt. As they look at "what is there now," they question "what was there before"; thus, their essays include historical information, before-and-after photos, and commentary from long-time residents and recent immigrants to illustrate transformations the students are beginning to record. Second, as the students blend their primary research with secondary scholarship, they discover the conversations taking place about their chosen site and begin to situate themselves within that discussion. Often surprised that academic research is available on their topic, students begin to recognize the significance of their inquiry. One student, for example, sure that no information would be available about golf courses, was surprised to discover reporting on both the previous use of the land and the complications involved in the current water rights. Third, perhaps the most important development is how, for many students, the audience has shifted from the classroom to many venues beyond it. Students' families, church members, townspeople, and employers have asked the students to share their writing. In some cases, people who began as interviewees have become active participants in the research and publication process, as when respondents to one student's investigation of a hiking trail's use encouraged her to post summaries of her findings about hiking/biking etiquette and safety along the trail.

A striking example of a student reaching public audiences was Erika, who lives in a small rural town in North Georgia. Her observational research initially focused on the only four public buildings in her town. When the townspeople became aware that she was writing an essay about their community, many contacted Erika to demonstrate their interest in her project, which prompted her to collect stories from each resident. The residents' letters, poems, historical anecdotes, and essays arrived in her mailbox for weeks. This town of 300 did not have an historian until Erika became the preserver of their stories. In addition, students who have analyzed their workplaces have incorporated their essays and photos into brochures, demonstrations, and public notices. One student's final project was adapted as an introductory portfolio for potential clients of a child development center. A young woman's analysis of the children's section of her local library became part of a demonstration in that facility.

Students Composing with an Eye to Visual Culture

Besides encouraging our students to develop a more self-consciously critical stance toward their environment, the work of reading visual culture prepares them to create their own writing products incorporating multimedia elements—i.e., integrating the verbal and the visual.

Photography has proven to be an invaluable starting point. Students have created "before and after" visual records, for example, showing the rapid shift of farmlands, open fields, or tree-filled hills to parking lots. But students have also found ways to tell positive pictorial stories about suburban life—the playground in one neighborhood where moms and young children regularly gather; the "make more green space" project claiming a longtime farm for a park rather than a new strip mall; soccer players and their appreciative audience of parents from a host of countries, simultaneously embodying and resisting the stereotype of "soccer mom."

Our initial work on using photos to present an argument asks students to do "pre-writing" or brainstorming about a single image they might produce—one photograph that could stand alone to tell a story and/or present an argument about the changing Atlanta suburbs. Students read "Learning to Trust the Last Picture on the Roll" from *The Subject is Research* to see how developing a strategic focus for a single photographic image can be analogous to narrowing down from subject to specific topic and then to an argument—whether in printed writing or visual narrative. At the same time, in class and in a course listserv, students can be discussing possible plans for taking and presenting their own single-photo story. For instance, when reading and responding to each others' planning, Sarah's spring 2003 composition students began to identify links between issues we had read about in scholarship on suburban life and visual imagery they had been encountering every day—but perhaps not yet interrogating critically. (See appendix for excerpts from online conversations.)

Students' formal presentations on such images have convinced us of photography's power to tell community stories, and also of students' abilities to use verbal text (oral and written) to interpret those stories with great sophistication. An even more important goal, however, has been to have our students combine images with print text—both writing they produce themselves and text selected strategically from a range of sources. In that vein, we agree with Howells that "we should not abandon verbal or literary analysis in favour of the visual" (4). In asking students to integrate print text with visual images, we are signaling our belief that both types are important and that they can work in complementary ways. To address this point instructionally, we begin with a relatively straightforward assignment asking students to juxtapose a single image or small group of images with an excerpt from a secondary reading. (See appendix for a copy of the assignment.) After these "starter" products, we are ready to move toward the composition of a multigenre writing project that integrates inscribed texts with images to present an argument about community life. (See Romano.)

By the time students are preparing their multigenre projects on community life, they have become thoroughly familiar with concepts from visual culture studies. At this point, in fact, most of them find that their drafting and revising processes can be facilitated by critiquing particular examples of hybrid compositions that make especially effective use of images (e.g., television news stories, *National Geographic* articles, and nonfiction books blending photos and illustrations with reporting and creative writing). Reading like writers, students identify strategies for setting up productive rhetorical relationships between verbal and visual texts, then apply those techniques in their own products. Some even choose to read theoretical discussions of visual culture, such as Richard Howells' analysis of websites as rhetorical spaces capitalizing on "integration, interaction, and impermanence" (232), his suggestions for unpacking ideological strands in new media texts (244), or his questions about documentary representation versus artistry in photographic images (160-64). Along the way, our discussions—whether by the whole class or in writing groups—continue to focus on students' daily encounters with visual culture—e.g., the new cars just bought on one student's street, the historic home being torn down for a parking lot, the flyers promoting course registration, even the buildings going up on campus. Meanwhile, students are creating their own hybrid compositions to present a forceful argument about community life: they are integrating printed verbal material with image-rich visual components and oral presentation. Their research and their arguments have been steeped in analysis of visual culture— whether arguing (via photos) that the playground space created for one new subdivision tells the story of its anticipated residents' aspirations, or that a two-mile stretch of road linking a town's restored Main Street with new chain stores embodies the tension between heritage and change. Taken together, their diverse multigenre projects show how far our students have come, both in their understanding of community as a socially constructed space and in their ability to see visual culture as contributing to that construction process. For instance, one student created a "sixth-grade student book bag" as a final project. The contents of this multigenre text illustrated the stressors and supports in the fictional middle schooler's life. The bag included a newsletter from a guidance counselor's office, a report card, a personal journal, and photos of family members. To challenge censorship trends emerging in response to a theater group's productions, one student created a hybrid text combining multiple visual and verbal elements: a playbill, a storyboard, a script, letters to the town newspaper, and a statement by the director of a play that had sparked local controversy.

Interpreting Classroom "Snapshots" and Planning Curriculum

While our students are busy using visual culture analysis to interpret community life, more and more we find ourselves calling on similar strategies to examine the classroom itself as a visible social environment. Especially when we meet to share stories about what we've been doing—both informally by the photocopying machine and more formally as when writing this essay together—we are often painting verbal snapshot moments of our classrooms. We describe such visual community moments as how students arranged their chairs for a discussion or how they interacted during oral presentations. These conversations, in turn, have led the two of us to brainstorm together about ways of bringing visual culture even more to the forefront in our course planning. We see an analogy, in fact, between our talk-through re-visitings of classroom snapshot moments—especially our shared speculations about how we might re-sequence and re-focus a particular instructional sequence next time—and the processes many of our students are using as they planned their multi-genre projects. (Students often described themselves as "laying out" the various visual elements of their papers at home and then re-vising.) Now we are trying to consider ways that we might make our ongoing reflections on social interactions in the classroom more visible to our students, so that they can join our efforts to use visual culture analysis as a way of improving our shared learning spaces.

In that spirit, at our invitation, our students made very helpful contributions to the specific work of this essay. Several students in Sarah's composition course (English 1102, honors) read a draft and provided both global and detailed responses. In addition, both of us benefited from students' discussions of course content as we were drafting and revising the essay. One set of students for each of us agreed to be videotaped during a class session to provide additional data about connections between visual culture studies and their writing of multigenre papers.

By combining community studies with analysis of visual culture, we can see that every time students gather chairs around a table for discussion or list revision notes for each other on a white board, they are composing more than papers for a course grade: they are helping to construct their own learning community. They are developing habits of mind that promote civic participation toward re-envisioning communities beyond the classroom.

Reflection

The collaborative experience of composing this essay within an inquiry community yielded important benefits for our teaching and our work as scholars. Our collaboration was multi-faceted—as a two-person writing team, within a small peer response group (with Renee Kaplan) and as part of a community of practice sponsored by our National Writing Project site. These multiple layers of collaboration all contributed simultaneously to our writing process and what we learned from it.

In the beginning, George Seaman's assembling teachers to reflect on professional practices encouraged us to think about possible topics we might write about together. We had been part of Keeping and Creating American Communities, another team of about two dozen educators developing interdisciplinary writing curricula grounded in the study of community life. Since collaboration had been such a productive part of the KCAC program, it seemed as if writing a collaborative essay about our teaching would be a logical next step.

The specific topic for the essay grew out of a presentation we did together for a regional conference on college-level teaching. In that presentation, we shared examples of how our students were learning to critique visual representations of New South culture and incorporating visual imagery into their compositions. While audience members seemed excited about the particular classroom strategies we shared, once we began to "translate" the presentation into an essay, we discovered many gaps in our thinking. Writing the essay together—especially with ongoing feedback and questions from our writing group member Renee—forced us to think more critically about the relationship between visual culture analysis and the conceptual framework for community studies that was evolving in KCAC classrooms.

Given that the essay began as an oral presentation, it may not be surprising that the first step in our writing process was to talk through the outline of that conference session. However, talk stayed at the center of our composing process throughout, more than we initially expected. We regularly got together with the plan of working on the essay, and then we would wind up talking throughout the meeting, rarely typing anything out, but instead discussing specific scenes from our classrooms and analyzing them in conversation. These discussions often led us to revise our essay's structure and content, at the same time as we theorized our teaching practices more explicitly. We left these sessions with rough notes for various segments of the essay, with each of us agreeing to draft certain portions. We would email those drafts to each other, gradually building the essay from pieces into which we both inserted prose.

After we had some rough draft material, we devoted one entire meeting time to typing out the introductory paragraphs of the essay in a "we" voice. That voice seemed so authentic a representation of what we were both doing in our two separate classrooms that we decided to convert the whole essay into first person plural, even though we had started out with each of us drafting sections in an "I" voice focused on our individual classrooms. Interestingly, Renee later told us that she thought, upon reading our first full draft, that we were team-teaching—working every day together in the same classroom. Actually, the scenes in our essay are a synthesis of events and practices that we carried out in separate classes, but with a compatible vision. Eventually, neither one of us could tell who wrote which sections, who polished which sentences. And individual teaching practices had migrated across our classrooms to a greater extent too.

During this drafting stage, we noticed that we each had different writing strengths, so we tried to capitalize on those differences. Linda was great at recalling details, for example, while Sarah liked to think about the organizational plan for the essay. As we negotiated specific points like word choice, the interaction made both of us more conscious of style.

Meanwhile, Renee's questions—most often delivered in online responses to our drafts—were crucial to our revision. When she signaled that a particular teaching technique wasn't clear to her, we re-worded our descriptive designation for it and/or added examples. Later on in our revision phase, we were also reading essays by two other members of the larger inquiry group—Dede Yow and Vicki Walker. This reading across other groups led us to begin seeing ourselves as part of a broader community of scholarship. On a practical level, we drew specific ideas for re-organizing and polishing our narrative from those essays. Vicki's emphasis on the stages of her own classroom project on visual culture helped us re-organize our transitions to emphasize the sequence of learning in our courses. Dede's passion for our topic led us to work on emphasizing the rationale behind our decisions. Reading their texts, in other words, added new, improved material to ours.

In a more ongoing way, we have changed the way we read others' writing about teaching. We still look for particular strategies that we can use in our classrooms, but now we also interrogate other authors' research approaches, try to un-pack their writing processes, connect their findings to other publications, and consider the implications of their work for our own future scholarship. Equally important, reading other essays while we were revising, and reading others' responses to our drafts, encouraged us to clarify and more self-consciously enact the principles behind our teaching practices. For one thing, since we had become so convinced of the value of "talk time" for our own writing, we realized our students could benefit from similar opportunities. We started to devote more class time to discussion of research planning and brainstorming of topics. We also began to use activities such as whole-group status checks on our students' writing processes; classroom "talk time" became more focused and deliberate. Another benefit this essay writing brought to our teaching was an effort to make our own decision-making processes and guiding philosophies clearer to our students. We moved from having a hodge-podge of techniques for linking visual culture with community studies to a conceptual framework with a purposeful sequence of learning activities. More specifically, we can now identify, with our students, the ways in which culture is imbedded in the material world—things we see (or fail to see fully) every day. And we plan purposeful sequences of activities to carry students from observing to analyzing to writing culture themselves. Perhaps most important, our work on this essay has enhanced our commitment to collaborative authorship in the classroom. We've both become more committed to our students' collaborating at all stages of their research and composing processes.

Appendix

Online Discussions by Students Planning Their Initial Photo Assignment

From Ashlee

I am planning to take pictures at the site for a planned city. The project is known as Canyon at Overlook and is a major development plan.... Most of you are looking to the past, but a major part of the Cartersville area has yet to be developed. If you would like to see pictures and more info, see this website: http://www.canyonatoverlook.com/

From Matt

While driving to a place I play paintball at (up past Woodstock, GA) I drive down a little road that still has farms and older buildings and even a little old outpost. I was thinking of taking pictures of this rundown outpost because it shows what Georgia used to be like....The other place I wanted to take pictures of is the subdivision next to my friend's house. There is a lot of land that has been plowed and started to be worked on to make a big community, and it's located right next to a new Golf Course and Subdivision. It shows that we are constantly building and it also compares the older houses to the newer ones being built....I could visit it twice a month and keep taking photographs of the progress the workers are making.

From Anthony

I'd like to take a picture of the tennis courts ... in my neighborhood. What is a better expression of suburban culture than a sporting universe next door? However, I also thought of taking pictures of cars. After all, in most people's minds, suburbia = wealth = nice cars. I think I'd like to wrestle with the whole mental image of the rich white guy in his 50s driving a Benz or a Lexus.

Directions for "Suburban Images" Assignment

The goal of this assignment is for you to select an image of something you see as a part of your everyday life and turn it into part of an argument within a meaningful rhetorical context. Your argument should relate to your reading from *Crabgrass Frontier* by Kenneth Jackson, "Urban Sprawl" by John Mitchell, *Bowling Alone* by Robert Putnam, and/or "No Place Like Home" by David Guterson. It might reinforce one of those writers' ideas, resist something they said, synthesize several key points, or present an alternative, more complex view of one of the issues explored in those readings. Your argument will be constructed through a combination of visual image and verbal text. In other words, you will write interpretive material to go along with your image. Your interpretive material should be partially **explanatory**: it should identify where you found the image and what is "going on" there in literal terms (i.e., provide a kind of when, where, how, and why for the image). Your interpretive material should also include a component that is **creative and dialogic**—that speaks *to, about, against, into* or *out of* the image using a *different genre of writing than explanation or description*. You might, for instance, find or write a poem that illuminates the image. You might append a short oral history from someone who appears in the image. You might tell a brief "imaginary" (or historical) story about the image. Finally, as suggested above, you should have a piece of text that is **relational**—that sets your image and writing in conversation with one of our secondary readings somehow. You might blend this piece into your explanation—for instance, by summarizing a key point from a secondary reading and then responding to it, or even by quoting a passage you want to affirm or resist with your image.

Besides thinking about what you want to include for each element in this hybrid presentation of visual and verbal material, you should think about your COMPOSITION choices—about *what goes where* and *why* in your presentation display. Medium of presentation should be another purposeful decision. You might want to set this up as a "word document" with the image imbedded in it. You might want to create a series of PowerPoint slides. You might want to create a web page or pages. Select a medium you are fairly confident using and one that seems to fit your subject and material well.

Most important of all: have fun doing the assignment and find a way to say something provocative, useful, entertaining, informative, or exciting about the Atlanta suburbs today.

Rubric

Possible points   Points earned

(10)   1.   appropriate subject for image and high quality image   _____

(10)   2.   detail and style of explanatory information about image   _____

(20)   3.   apt reference/relating to topic/issue from secondary reading(s)   _____

(20)   4.   striking and content-effective "creative" verbal element(s)   _____

(20)   5.   overall design of presentation/display   _____

(20)   6.   unity and effectiveness of total package's argument   _____

_____   TOTAL   _____

References

American Beauty. Dir. Sam Mendes. Perf. Kevin Spacey and Annette Benning. 1999. Videocassette. DreamWorks Home Entertainment, 1999.

Ballenger, Bruce. "Learning to Trust the Twelfth Picture on the Roll." *The Subject is Research: Processes and Practice*. Ed. Wendy Bishop and Pavel Zemliansky. Portsmouth: Boynton/Cook/Heinemann, 2001. 28-42.

Beuka, Robert. "Just One Word… 'PLASTICS'." *The Journal of Popular Film and Television* 28 (2000): 12-22.

The Graduate. Dir. Mike Nichols. Perf. Anne Bancroft and Dustin Hoffman. Videocassette. MGM/UA Studios, 2001.

Howells, Richard. *Visual Culture*. Cambridge: Blackwell Press, 2003.

Jackson, Kenneth T. *Crabgrass Frontier: The Suburbanization of the United States*. New York: Oxford UP, 1987.

Jay, Martin. "Cultural Relativism and the Visual Turn." *Journal of Visual Culture* 1 (2002): 267-78.

Keeping and Creating American Communities. 2001. KCAC. 20 April 2003 <http://kcac.kennesaw.edu>.

Lippard, Lucy. *The Lure of the Local: Senses of Place in a Multicentered Society*. New York: New Press, 1998.

"Monty Can't Buy Me Love." *The Simpsons*. By John Swartzwelder. Dir. Mark Ervin. Fox. 2 May 1999.

Romano, Tom. *Blending Genre, Altering Style: Writing Multigenre Papers*. Portsmouth: Boynton/Cook, 2000.

Say Anything. Dir. Cameron Crowe. Perf. John Cusak, Ione Skye, and John Mahoney. 1989. Videocassette. 20th Century Fox Home Entertainment, Inc., 1989.

Stock, Patricia Lambert. "The Function of Anecdote in Teacher Research." *English Education* 25 (1993): 173-187.

Sunshine State. Dir. John Sayles. Perf. Jane Alexander, Angela Bassett, Gordon Clapp, and Edie Falco. 2002. Videocassette. Columbia Pictures Industries, Inc., 2002.

Part III

☙

Writing Group Three:
Designing Writing Programs

Social Revision

Victoria Walker, Leslie Walker, and Andy Smith

Our writing group was in a unique position in relation to the others involved in our larger inquiry community because we each came to the project with drafts of our essays in hand. All of us had previously attended an Advanced Writing Institute at our National Writing Project site, where we had written the initial versions of our essays. Therefore, when we joined the new writing group assembled as part of this project's community, we first had to establish a comfort level with our new readers—a step which required letting go of the strong sense of ownership we were already feeling for our drafts.

This crucial step involved getting to know each other better before immersing ourselves in shared revision. Although we had spent time together during previous NWP programs, we had never had the opportunity to work together on the more intimate level that a writing group requires. Before we could feel comfortable sharing our writing, we had to build a level of trust that led us into becoming a team of writers. It was after we reached that familiarity that we were able to work together on refining our essays.

In hindsight, we think it's important that all three of us recognized and explicitly strategized ways of addressing the need to establish a trusting community first. At the time, we didn't take note of the fact that this move was such a big part of what made our work successful. But now, in retrospect, we realize that one factor enabling our group was a shared belief in collaboration—a value fostered in part by our NWP site affiliation. Specifically, all of us already had a sense of belonging to a larger writing community of teachers, and that made establishing this new small group easier.

In any case, we first set out to create a comfortable atmosphere for sharing our writing. This effort included seemingly simple but important things such as choosing central meeting places that had a social feel (e.g., restaurants on a town square). At the start of our sessions, we would devote time to getting to know each other better beyond the context of our writing task, and we even explicitly noted ways we were doing so, such as sharing stories from our home life. Overall, we devoted substantial time during our meetings to creating a deep mutual respect for each other's work and for ourselves as people as well as professionals. As a result of this commitment, we became increasingly comfortable presenting our thoughts and writing to the group, because each of us trusted that we would be heard with an understanding ear.

While building a comfortable space for interaction was crucial, so were other protocols more directly linked to the revision process. One rule we set early on was PQP—praise, question, polish. This positive approach to giving constructive criticism affirmed our commitment to valuing each other as well as the work. We always began by pointing to strengths in the piece we were discussing before moving on to asking questions and making suggestions for improvement.

Another protocol that we established was exchanging our drafts via email before our get-togethers. Typically, we sent our drafts to each other at least a week before the writing group meeting. This strategy gave us a chance to read the material carefully before the in-person discussions, thus having the chance to formulate a thoughtful response ahead of time.

Interestingly, although we had studied the drafts before our meetings, we still read them aloud once we came together as a group, and we responded verbally to those readings, even if we had made margin notes as well. At the end of the meeting, we would pass along the copies, with our notes, to the essay author. A related practice that yielded major benefits was talking through ideas in a global, exploratory way, including considering philosophical questions about teaching. In this case, our broad-based discussions led us to recognize that all three of us were writing about writing programs—how to design and refine them. Seeing this common framework in our pieces helped us to new thinking about our individual essays and about our teaching practices.

One other key protocol we used was to end each meeting by thinking together about what was accomplished—what made the discussion successful and/or unsuccessful. Reflecting out loud, explicitly, on this point led us to continually refine our practices for sharing and also carried over into other venues. (Along those lines, in the summer of 2005, when Andy and Vicki team-taught a week-long staff development course for a school district, they were able to draw on their formative evaluations of their own writing group's protocols to shape the planning for establishing writing groups in their class.)

Looking back, we realize that the protocols we used, in and of themselves, were important. Because we did things like sharing drafts before meetings, and because we established predictable patterns for responding (like the PQP), we knew what to expect. As a result, our group meetings ran efficiently, and we maintained our comfort level with each other and with the process.

Sharing our work led each of us to valuable "ah-ha" moments, both in our individual pieces of writing and in our ability to use writing groups in other contexts. One of the many positive aspects of working with a small writing group is that the members of the group begin to gain a sense of shared ownership for all the composing being done in the group. Ideas generated in the group stimulate reflection and revision. Now, Andy says, he understands the need to always have "another set of eyes to help you out." And Leslie points to her realization that all writers share a common bond—that they can relate to each other on the basis of how challenging writing can be. With that in mind, while we've used different specific practices in other groups we've joined since this one, we are always careful to set up and continually refine protocols for managing the process of sharing and responding. For instance, when Vicki enrolled in a graduate program in professional writing, she drew on her experience in our writing group to offer suggestions for how her classmates could workshop effectively. And when she later joined a writing group of professional authors from outside school, she immediately felt comfortable because of her experiences with our group.

The knowledge we have gained from working in this small writing group has proven to be invaluable to our teaching as well. After collaborating over a period of time with our group, we understood our teaching better and were able to reflect upon and revise our work in the classroom just as we revise and edit our writing. As Leslie says, this work is "never done."

Perhaps most important, participating in this particular group—one in which all three of us successfully refined writing about our teaching of writing—led us to appreciate the power of writing groups as havens for learning. Our small reflective group was a protected, semi-public forum where, as authors, we were able to gauge the response of some supportive readers before bringing our writing into a more public light. As we move these essays from that protected forum, we feel confident about doing so because our group helped us see ourselves as good writers with something valuable to say to other educators. We now view ourselves in a different professional light than in the past. Vicki may have said it best: "I feel that by writing about my teaching and talking about my writing with other professionals, I have gained a deeper understanding of my practice and my philosophy of teaching. I have gained passion, and more importantly, I have the conviction and the knowledge to back up my teaching." For all of us, the source of this new confidence in ourselves was the work of our group. We were able to give each other genuine help with our writing, and through that process we all opened our eyes to the power of collaboration.

Picture This: Using Wordless Books to Teach Primary-Grade Writers

Victoria Walker
Compton Elementary School

"Can we truly teach primary students to write?"

I was sitting with my colleague Ann, in an elementary classroom, at a table sized for the average six-year-old. A stack of writing portfolios loomed between us as she anxiously posed this question to me. We were discussing how her first graders were able to label their pictorial representations of stories with one or two words, or to write patterned sentences in the vein of "I like my mom," "I like my dad," "I like my dog." Although this is certainly considered writing in primary classrooms, it is a far leap from the type of writing that relays a story. Ann felt her students were strong in reading and sounding out words, but their progress in applying these skills in their writing was at a standstill. She wondered how we could help them move beyond pictures, labeling, and patterned sentences and into what we were considering true writing: a series of sentences that would reveal a progression of events. Perhaps the simple form of communication that the students were producing was as far as the average first grader was conceptionally ready to venture, and we should be happy that they were making attempts at writing. But Ann was discouraged because she believed that they were capable of writing more words that would tell a story. Could we teach them to write in the way that writers do? We decided we would try to find out. We started brainstorming ways we could combine the picture labels with the sentences and foster sequential story telling that would lead them to put all these skills together, becoming real writers.

We were already providing many varied opportunities for writing practice. Beyond Writing Workshop, the students had engaged in dictating their words, whole-group interactive writing, journal writing, and open-ended writing centers. In his book *Ways of Seeing*, John Berger reminds us that as a child develops, "Seeing comes before words. The child looks and recognizes before it can speak." Therefore, we can easily deduce that, developmentally, pictures would come to a child before words. This is exactly what we were experiencing with these students. Most of their independent writing consisted of drawing elaborate pictures and orally explaining a detailed occurrence of one event. Moreover, as is the norm with children of this age, the actual words they had been writing to accompany these pictures consisted of two or three words, such as "My dog," that served as a label for the pictures. We agreed that we needed to teach them to tell a complete story and in the process expand their ability to produce written words. Thus, our journey began in the fall and continued throughout the course of the year.

I was in a unique position, as I was not bound to the same group of students the entire day. As a special assignment teacher, I had the privilege of working with six different classes of primary students ranging from kindergarten to second grade in the areas of reading and writing and was privy to seeing the developmental progression of ages five to eight unfold. From watching the students of each level, I had gained a sense of where the students could go academically. I was teaching children of middle to low socioeconomic status in a school of approximately nine hundred students located just outside the city of Atlanta. We harbored children of diverse ethnic backgrounds from all ability levels. I additionally had the benefit of collaborating with some talented teachers, such as Ann, learning new ideas and gaining the freedom to try some of my own within their classrooms. The word got around quickly that I enjoyed teaching writing and had some innovative ideas. Beginning with Ann's question, a narrative-making program for teaching writing evolved.

As Ann and I talked, our goals began to emerge. We decided that we wanted the students to be active participants in writing processes as identified by Donald Graves in *Writing: Teachers and Children at Work*. The Georgia Core Curriculum in all primary grades states that students take part in the writing process, and we believed this was a good start. More importantly, we wanted the students to gain a sense of the individual process they follow to construct their writing, as well as to study specific authoring techniques. We also wanted the students to build a strong story-telling base by understanding that each narrative has a beginning, middle, and end and to apply this understanding when writing their own narratives. Ann invited me to work with the first graders in her classroom, thus giving me a chance to try some new techniques that could be shared with other teachers as well. I decided to approach writing instruction by building on the skills the students already possessed, using literature as a model, and then moving them into expanding their writing of text from this point.

I noticed in working with these first grade students that they drew beautiful pictures with a great amount of detail to represent the story to be told. After drawing, most students orally performed the story in elaborate detail among their peers or to the teacher. Ann and I realized that they had a sense of oral narrative that was ahead of what they could produce in print.

In *Images in Language, Media, and Mind* Roy Fox points out that a growing trend recognizes the importance of images in developing literacy. He cites the research of Janet Emig, who found that students naturally rely on nonlinguistic modes of thinking while composing. According to her research, writing and thinking should not be taught as isolated sub- skills, but together as part of an interchangeable process. With this goal of the meshing images and print, I wanted to preserve children's wonderful enthusiasm and skill, but shape it to meet our writing goals. It seemed imperative to tap into that skill of oral narrative mastery as a starting point. Often when reproducing thoughts in print, the students became lost in representing the sounds and words, at the expense of the story. I had an idea: why not free up the students by temporarily taking out the text factor so that they could pictorially write and gain a sense of narration and authorship? Let them tell their stories in pictures while experimenting with the use of structure. We could use this foundation to build up to representing ideas with print. I wanted to motivate these early writers to take that first step towards authorship and to feel successful so that they would continue to write. Building on their skills as artists and oral storytellers would facilitate my goal.

The genre of literature that would be used as a model for our young writers would clearly be wordless picture books. These are books that tell the story through pictures, without print text. In *Wondrous Words: Writers and Writing in the Elementary Classroom,* Katie Wood Ray discusses the idea of students reading like writers. Instead of reading solely for the story itself, Ray maintains that we must teach writing students to read also for the purpose of studying the techniques used in the writings of others. Observing authors' techniques gives the students models and tools that they can apply to enhance their writing. Since I was building on their skills as artists and storytellers, wordless books would drive instruction. I would lead the students into reading a wordless book as if they were authors. Our writing would be an opportunity to apply these learned techniques after they gained a sense of the story and the process.

Deciding on a study of wordless books and author techniques was the beginning of meeting our writing goals for these first graders. Our idea was that after we built a strong foundation of story structure and writing processes using wordless books, then we would study additional genres of literature and represent our stories with text as students grew in writing and phonemic awareness. We would work to make this progression through much guidance and modeling. The hope was eventually to change the balance from pictures, to pictures and text. We created our own curriculum, learning as we went. I used wordless books as a starting place to build a sense of story structure, writing process, and techniques. Creating this sense of design was part of an ongoing process to teach effective writing.

Getting Started With the Practice

I began with the children's need to collect and monitor their work. For organizational purposes, I secured two folders for each student. The first was for keeping work in progress together. The second was for collecting all finished writings once each piece had been celebrated in the classroom for a respectful period of time. This folder would serve as a portfolio of works completed so that the students could reflect on previous work for technique, and so that they could track their own personal growth as writers throughout the year. It would also serve to assess and determine whether the students were progressing towards our goals.

Launching into my first intense study of wordless books as a writer meant that I had to become a collector of books from this particular genre. Wordless books are categorized under the larger umbrella of picture books, which means that when searching for books under this category they may or may not contain text. This general categorization makes it difficult to specifically filter out the books that represent the story through pictures alone although there are an abundance of these texts available. I looked through libraries and bookstores, browsing through books and reading descriptions in book catalogues. I searched under the leading booksellers online and additionally found a number of wordless books in our school's kindergarten curriculum materials.

Once I built up a sufficient collection, the teacher cleared a special space to display these books in her classroom. It is my belief that learners tend to become engaged with what they are already familiar with. I think all students have experiences that they bring to a new learning opportunity. These experiences are what they use as a foundation for new learning. Thus, I wanted the first graders to browse through these books independently to build experiences with the books and form some ideas about them prior to my instruction.

Engaging the Students

I chose *Pancakes for Breakfast* by Tommie DePaola for our first experience because the pictures are drawn frame by frame in a linear pattern where the action is obvious. The students already knew this author's work. The group sat before me on the floor as I held the book up for all the students to see while I was reading the title and author. I briefly explained that this was a book meant for us to read the pictures to understand the story. Some students were excited that they had seen the book. My intention for this initial sharing was for the students to first experience the book for the story itself while being exposed to this type of picture writing. I "storied" the book for the students, orally recounting the action depicted in each frame as the plot unfolded. The students added comments periodically, but the reading was mainly my explaining the picture sequence to the students. As we reached the end of the book, I suggested that since they were such wonderful artists, it would be interesting for us to each create a wordless story like Tommie DePaola did, thus starting them to think about using the author as a model for writing style. We agreed from previous workshop experiences that we needed to do some prewriting, gathering information and generating ideas. I gave students a piece of paper folded into sections. I instructed them to write or draw in each frame a favorite topic such as family and friends, foods, a special trip. Each student began a personal process of creating a wordless story.

From Reading to Writing

In the next session, I once again brought out the wordless book *Pancakes for Breakfast* and was met with some excitement, a few groans, and the comment that we "did that one yesterday." This was my sure lead! I explained that when we previously read the book, we were reading to understand and enjoy the story. Since we wanted to write wordless stories of our own, we were going to look at this book once more to study how Tommie DePoala created his story. Again, I read the author and title on both the cover and title page, setting up a ritual for beginning a book. As I started reading the story, I realized that a difference this time was that I wasn't reading the book alone. The students were raising their hands and in turn telling the story that they had merely observed the day before. I went to great lengths to point out how the pictures told the story and encouraged the students as they read to pull out the important details that helped us understand the sequence of the events. We discussed the fact that, although the setting was the same in a sequence of pictures, some part of the frame was changed to show the action progressing. We found examples of techniques such as facial expressions, think bubbles, and objects in the pictures that the author used to convey to us what was occurring in the story. Then we storied a second wordless book, Changes by Pat Hutchins, in the same way. We were reading from the perspective of a writer studying not only the story, but as authors looking from the perspective of writing. As the students were engaging in this new perspective in reading, I brought up the idea that all stories have a beginning, middle, and ending. We identified these parts in each of the wordless stories we had already encountered. I took a piece of paper folded into three parts and modeled this idea with my own picture representations by showing three stages of the building of a snowman. I then solicited the class to name additional techniques I could use that may make my wordless story more understandable to the reader. I received some suggestions, and modeled how to add these to my story. I suggested that the students look back at the idea sheets from our previous session to help them think of a subject for their own three-part story. Each student received a paper folded into three parts just like my model and began writing their own three-part picture story.

As we moved through the next few writing sessions, our practice became to story a new wordless book prior to our actual writing block and to discuss the sequence of events as well as the techniques the author of the featured book used to convey the story. For example, we read The Birthday Present by Mavis Smith. It had some words that were part of the street signs in the story. I pointed out how they were important to the pictures, but they didn't tell the story. I suggested that while a wordless book tells the story in pictures, a writer could certainly use words if they were important to the picture and help the reader understand the action. I noticed this technique surfacing in some drafts soon after. One student applied this idea very well. In the story of her mother's birthday party, she drew a banner in her picture that read "HAPPY BIRTHDAY MOM!"—clearly important to the story but not telling the story itself. In the same vein, another student added a "PIZZA DELIVERY" sign to the top of a car to explain his story of ordering pizza. Finally, one student became very animated about his pictures remaining in black and white after we studied a book featuring this technique. The students were beginning to experiment with book techniques to build narrative structure.

Conferencing With Students

As the three-part drafts of wordless stories began to take shape, the need for writing conferences surfaced. Most teachers of writing have a personal style for organizing student conferencing. Since the classroom teacher and I were both circulating around the room, we found the simplest way for us, at the beginning, was to hold informal conferences as the students needed help, while making sure we reached each student before the draft was completed.

We asked students to explain their three-part pictures and tell how the story progressed from beginning, to middle, to end. Narrative structure was our primary goal in the early conferences. If the story was confusing or lacked sequence, I asked the students to explain how they wanted the story to progress and then asked questions that would lead them to discover a natural sequence. I helped the students recall author techniques to help the sequence flow. In some cases the first, second, and third picture had no common thread. I had a conference with one student who had a picture of two people in a swimming pool for the first frame, then a terrific thunderstorm in the next frame. It seemed to me as she narrated the events that two different stories were in progress. I suggested that she choose one theme and follow it throughout the story. As we discussed her ideas, she decided that she would draw her friend arriving on a sunny day to swim, then move the picture of the children swimming to the second frame. Finally, the third frame depicted the storm, but she decided to add a drawing of an empty swimming pool to show that the children had to abandon their plans as a result of the storm, a technique of repeating pictures that she had recalled from a previous wordless book.

In some cases we needed to give the student specific suggestions. Another student was skilled at drawing motorcycles, and naturally as a result had the same motorcycle in each of his three frames. In this case I asked the student to explain his story, and together we decided that he didn't have one. We discussed possible ideas for a motorcycle story, and I suggested that something could happen to the original motorcycle in his beginning that would make it look different in the end. The next day as I was walking by his table, I was excited to see that his story showed a motorcycle with a nail in the tire.

Through these early teacher/writer conferences, Ann and I found that it worked well to ask the students to tell the story orally so that we could better understand their thought processes before giving suggestions. It was crucial to help students to remember to focus on one idea or theme and to follow through with a beginning, middle and end. The conference focused on suggestions for helping the reader understand the story and its action. It was important to make suggestions and not demands, as Lucy Calkins advocates in *The Art of Teaching Writing*. She maintains that teachers of growing writers should follow this simple sequence: first be fully present as a listener to the writer, learning everything we can so that we can obtain the information to best help the writer. The next step is to ask questions about the piece that will help the writer make the story clear, and then finally to make suggestions. We wanted to honor the efforts of the author by only giving suggestions.

As the students continued their drafts, we checked their progress to make sure that they were on target as the stories developed. The students sat at tables of four to five, which gave them a chance to discuss their work with each other too. As the students storied their drafts for us and developed a sequential three-part wordless story, Ann and I presented them with three separate sheets to transfer the draft into the beginnings of a final copy. Conferences became increasingly more formal, focusing on editing and fine-tuning as well as making sure all the parts of the book were in place.

The Process of Creating the Product

Once each student had a solid three-part picture narrative draft, it was time to transfer the idea into a more formal copy. Here began a rewriting stage. I gave each student three pieces of paper to redraw their three-part wordless story, with each part (beginning, middle, and end) on its own sheet. On this drawing, they were charged to consider additional detail that could be added to their original pictures to help the reader understand how the story progressed. We continued to work on three-part wordless narratives, and the students had conferences with both teachers and with their peers. Again, we gave help in the form of suggestions, and the students became the final authority of their work.

I continued to feature a published wordless book at the beginning of each session, reading first for pleasure, and then reading as writers to study the techniques of the author and relate these ideas to our own work. The sharing of the wordless narratives switched from being teacher-centered to student-centered, as I began to step away from narrating the book with the students providing the comments, to letting the students become the ones to story the book. I became the facilitator interjecting as necessary to help our understanding and discussion to flow, but the narration and talk were the students' own. I found it most productive in these wordless book sessions to choose one student at a time to story a succession of two pages, switching narrators as we turned the pages so that most students would have a turn. My reason was twofold: First, it gave the students a sense of audience and practice narrating to an audience so that they would become aware that there were actual readers of the story. It additionally served classroom management purposes to keep all students engaged in the story and the discussion.

On one occasion, we were scheduled to study Raymond Briggs's *The Snowman*, a beautifully drawn classic wordless book with multiple story frames and much detail. Ann and I made the decision to use this book with small independent groups so that the students could get a closer look at the pictures. After securing multiple copies from the school, public library, and personal collections, we gave a copy to each group of four students. We gave with it specific directions to story the book within their group, taking turns on pages as we would in a whole group discussion, and finishing with a brief report to the whole group. This was the real test. I wanted to see how well the students could follow the narrative of a wordless book and identify author techniques without a teacher facilitator. As I circulated the room during the small-group study, I noticed that most groups were engaged in the book, although I had to give a few gentle reminders on how to story a wordless book. In the end, the students generally seemed to have a good sense of the story and the techniques used to create it. I attributed the ability of the students to read the pictures and gain the understanding of the story to our daily practice with wordless stories.

The students were becoming increasingly proficient as readers and writers. These first graders were beginning to transfer their understanding of the stories' and authors' techniques, as well as writing process, to their own work. The students' final three-part wordless narratives were taking form, and it was time to begin featuring work in progress as examples during group discussion. It became the practice that after studying a published wordless book we would ask permission to show the work of a classmate, letting the student share the piece or choose to have me narrate it. We pointed out the techniques we noticed in the piece and the things that made the story work. The class started out unsure of how to comment on peer writing, and I had to model this at first. We were quick to point out when a student gave a comment or question that was on target. We then gave suggestions for what the student might do next and related those ideas to other students' work. This showcase of work in progress gave the students new ideas and examples of how their work should progress. Soon, students were asking to have their stories in progress featured before the class for comments, and we had to start a sign-up sheet.

During this time, we continued perfecting our three-part narratives as well as adding the necessary parts that would eventually transform our stories into a wordless book. Each day as we storied a wordless book, we looked at a different attribute that is common to all picture books and added it to our own wordless stories. We began with the cover and title page. In a whole-group session, I pointed out the title of our latest wordless book; we discussed if and why that title was a good one for the book and how it matched the theme of the story. I pointed out the author and illustrator that were named on the front of the book and on the inside title page as well. The students were then charged to create a cover and title page complete with author and illustrator named on the front for their own books. We continued this practice with the book dedication and the ending author page. For each mini-lesson we studied book parts and found them in some of the wordless books we had previously featured, then transferred them to our own wordless books. By the end of our study and writing of wordless books, each student was responsible for having a three-part wordless narrative, a cover and title page, a dedication, and an author page. Eventually all students had written, held conferences, edited, and finally produced the finished writing of a wordless book. They then put the books together and added the last part, the copyright.

Reading for the Public

By this time the goals we had for these first graders were beginning to be realized. Each student had been an active participant in a conventional writing process as well as gaining a sense of his or her own personal writing process and what it means individually to be a writer. The students were beginning to read as writers and now had under their belts the techniques of many accomplished wordless book authors and more importantly the skills necessary to identify and model techniques. These kindergarten writers had a sense of narrative structure. It was time for them to share their stories and celebrate the efforts it takes to become a writer and an author.

It was a special day. We called it our Author Celebration, and with it came an air of honor and accomplishment throughout the classroom. There was a special author's chair for the final reading of each featured author's book. Students could sit in the author's chair and story their wordless book before the class. Each student chose to share, with only one asking me to lead the sharing while he sat next to me and assisted. The classroom teacher and I modeled for the students how to be an audience during the author readings. This is the point where we realized that our educational beliefs, classroom practices, and reflection on what we hoped to accomplish all started coming together. Each author in turn storied his or her book for the class and afterwards took questions and comments about the finished book. Most of the books were clear and understandable, and numerous author techniques for wordless books were apparent. Each student had a three-part wordless story with a clear beginning, middle, and ending. The students had gained a solid sense of narrative structure. The best reward of all was that all students had a tremendous sense of pride. They now saw themselves as writers.

The End of the Beginning

At the end of an entire school year of practicing this approach, I found myself again sitting at the same classroom table with the same colleague, a stack of first-grade writing portfolios sitting between us. We were looking at the first wordless books the students had written and comparing them to the ones they had since undertaken on their own, as well as some pieces integrating images along with printed text. It was apparent that the wordless book study had facilitated their growth as writers. We reflected on the question that had plagued us many months ago and launched us into our search for a new approach: "Can you truly teach primary students to write?" We had found an answer: yes, you can!

There was one goal yet to be fully realized. The original dilemma we faced was how to teach these students to write with words as well as pictures, and we would spend the rest of the year working to this goal as our ideas for teaching beginning writing continued to evolve. Eventually Ann and I began using other genres of literature in the same way we had featured wordless books. Our purpose remained to move the students into writing text.

Creating wordless books was by no means intended to be an end within itself. It was a beginning, a place where the students had the opportunity to study authors and learn the structure, language, and craft associated with telling a story, as well as a place where they began to follow these conventions into becoming writers of text. Most importantly, it gave them a chance to practice writing in a non-threatening way. By the end of the year, most had moved into writing complete stories with a considerable amount of text.

As I revisit this experience now, I take pride in how well these first grade students succeeded. I have since tried this same approach with a multi-age primary class, and the students were successful. I've also tried my technique with two kindergarten classes, where some students were successful and others encountered major pitfalls. This setback taught me that students have to be ready to understand narrative and story structure. Previous instruction about narratives would have to build to this use of wordless books to teach writing.

It wasn't until I wrote about this experience and discussed it in open dialogue with teachers who work with older students that I began to fully understand the full extent of what I had been teaching. Sharing my ideas with colleagues helped clarify what I had been trying to accomplish. Instinct about what the students needed had led me to the right practices, but reflection and sharing my ideas helped me to thoroughly understand and grow. Now I realize through talking with other teachers that the thought processes and skills we were using were very complex. This realization explains to me why some groups struggled. They needed more of the basic knowledge about story to undertake the narrative process. In addition, I found from working with second and third graders later, and from talking to middle and high school teachers, that older grade levels could benefit from using wordless books to revisit narrative and story structure. Through sharing and reflection, I deepened my understanding of writing, just as my students had done.

Reflection

When I joined our book's inquiry community, I was eager to study reflection-in-action as practiced in writing groups. At an earlier four-week summer institute, I had written a rough draft of my essay on wordless books and writing instruction in the primary grades. After much discussion and writing with my initial group, I felt that I had my ideas about this teaching practice securely in place. However, I soon found that I still had more to learn, and the process of working in my new writing group definitely improved my essay and other writing I have done since then.

Leslie and Andy, my new readers, supported revision of my essay in several important ways—some focused on basic organization and presentation, some aimed at deepening the thinking behind my story. Reading Andy's essay—which had section headings already in place—led me to try that strategy for guiding my reader. In creating those headings, I had to think harder about my essay's organizational plan, and discussions in our group clarified my essay structure. Meanwhile, talking about Leslie's piece helped me flesh out the philosophy behind my pedagogy. My draft presented a step-by-step narrative of what I was doing in the classroom—a parallel to the straightforward narrative I was teaching my students to compose with pictures—but discussing Leslie's essay encouraged me to write about the rationale behind the teaching practices I was urging others to adopt.

While these talks with my new group took my essay to a new level, they also built my confidence as a teacher and writer. I began to feel that I had it in me to think and write as a professional. By thinking **through** *writing, I learned how to tap into the level of reflection that allowed me to put my philosophy into practice—both in teaching and in writing.*

Now I know that the more we educators reflect and discuss practices, the more we realize there is much to discover about teaching. This idea seems so simple that I don't know why it took me years to realize. Interestingly, it was only when I had to describe my classroom in language for my writing group that I began to see how what I was teaching was actually far more complex than I had realized. Being able to talk about my teaching with educators from other levels was especially rewarding. For example, my instincts had told me that my primary students needed a springboard to actual print, but it wasn't until I began verbalizing my thoughts to other teachers from high school and college settings, that the more complex concepts embedded in my teaching emerged for me. I wasn't merely leading students to begin using print. I was also teaching visual discrimination, narrative structure, and author techniques. My approach was helping primary students to synthesize and evaluate information: I was teaching the highest order of thinking skills. I found that my original ideas had more depth than I ever imagined and that they had applications for teaching students of all grade levels. (A response report from Linda

Stewart, a member of another one of our project's writing groups, was particularly helpful in pointing out these connections. See "Reading Across Writing Groups.")

Thinking about what I am doing for my students on so many levels beyond the isolated practice of using wordless books has helped me to be a better teacher. Now when I start a new unit, I make it a point to journal periodically throughout the unit so that I can reflect on and then see before me what is happening with the students in response to my teaching. As a unit progresses, I can look to my teaching journal for patterns in student learning to help me understand the learning taking place. I now meet regularly with the teachers on my team and we exchange ideas and trouble-shoot to find the best possible way to help our students. I feel empowered taking this approach because I am able to use shared reflection to find the best practices for our classrooms.

Overall, building on the learning in my writing group, I have become a more confident and effective teacher. In the classroom, instead of a hit-or-miss approach where I accidentally fall into the right practice but have little idea of why, I now work consciously to envision and articulate concepts as I teach. I fully explore what I want to accomplish and how I want to accomplish it. I don't believe that I could have achieved this level of self-reflection in my teaching today without the experience of writing and reflecting with my writing group. I know that my teaching now has greater passion and that I have both the conviction and the knowledge to back up my teaching claims.

My writing group and our whole community of practice had a profound effect on my abilities as a writer. Working with these colleagues gave me the confidence to apply for a graduate professional writing program, where I am one of the few elementary educators enrolled. Significantly, in that program, I've found that most of the other students have less experience with collaborative writing that I do. In and outside class, I have been able to offer suggestions about how to workshop effectively and to model some strategies learned from the writing groups in this project. Recently, I joined a well-established group of professional writers outside of my graduate program setting, and this new group easily accepted me as a peer.

Working on this essay as a member of an active community of practice has been invaluable. It exposed me to new ideas and writing techniques. It gave me confidence in myself as a teacher and a writer. The writing, the thinking, and the discussions helped me clarify my philosophy of teaching and learning. I now view my teaching from the perspective of a writer as well as a teacher: the two go hand in hand. My learning grew gradually from writing about a specific teaching practice that worked well for me, to revisiting the experience reflectively and refining my thinking in ways that will forever shape the way I teach. I now collaborate with my students through journaling and reflecting. I now understand that as long as I practice such social approaches to reflection, my story will never conclude—and the learning will never end.

References

Berger, John. *Ways of Seeing*. Boston: Bedford/St. Martin's, 2000.

Calkins, Lucy M. *The Art of Teaching Writing*. Portsmouth: Heinemann, 1986.

Depaola, Tommie. *Pancakes for Breakfast*. New York: Scholastic, 1978.

Fox, Roy F. *Images in Language, Media, and Mind*. Urbana: NCTE, 1994.

Graves, Donald. *Writing: Teachers and Children at Work*. Portsmouth: Heinemann, 1983.

Hutchins, Pat. *Changes, Changes*. New York: Scholastic, 1971.

Ray, Katie Wood. *Wondrous Words: Writers and Writing in the Elementary Classroom*. Urbana: NCTE, 1999.

Smith, Mavis. *The Birthday Present*. New York: Scholastic, 1994.

Wordless Books

Bang, Molly. *Gray Lady and the Strawberry Snatcher*. New York: Simon & Schuster, 1980.

Briggs, Raymond. *The Snowman*. New York: Random House, 1978.

Crews, Donald. *Truck*. New York: Greenwillow Books, 1987.

Day, Alexandra. *Carl's Birthday*. New York: Harper Collins, 1995.

---. *Good Dog Carl*. New York: Aladdin Paperbacks, 1985.

---. *The Christmas We Moved to the Barn*. New York: Harper Collins Juvenile Books, 1997.

DePaola, Tommie. *The Hunter and the Animals: A Wordless Picture Book*. New York: Holiday House, 1981.

---. *Pancakes for Breakfast*. New York: Scholastic, 1978.

Hutchins, Pat. *Changes, Changes*. New York: Scholastic, 1971.

Keats, Ezra Jack. *Clementia's Cactus*. New York: Viking, 1999.

Mayer, Mercer, and Marianna Mayer. *A Boy, A Dog, A Frog and a Friend*. New York: Dial Books for Young Readers, 1971.

Mayer, Mercer. *Frog Goes to Dinner*. New York: Dial Books for Young Readers, 1992.

McCully, Emily Arnold. *Picnic*. New York: Harper Collins, 1987.

Smith, Mavis. *The Birthday Present*. New York: Scholastic, 1994.

Spier, Peter. *Peter Spier's Rain*. New York: Yearling, 1997.

Rohmann, Eric. *Time Flies*. New York: Crown Publishers, 1994.

Ward, Lynd. *The Silver Pony: A Story in Pictures*. New York: Houghton Mifflin, 1973.

Wiesner, David. *Free Fall*. New York: William and Morrow, 1988.

Wiesner, David. *Tuesday Morning*. New York: Clarion Books, 1991.

Wilson, April. *April Wilson's Magpie Magic: A Tale of Colorful Mischief*. New York: Dial Books for Young Readers, 1999.

Re-envisioning the Writing Classroom

Leslie Walker
Campbell High School

A Classroom in Spring

"Order in the court! Order, please!" The judge pounds his gavel on the podium and waits for silence. "Mr. Foreman, has the jury reached a verdict?"

"Yes, we have your Honor. In the case The State of Scotland vs. Macbeth, we find the defendant, Macbeth, not guilty."

Pandemonium breaks loose in the courtroom. A spectator leaps over a desk and assassinates Macbeth. Some are covering their mouths in astonishment. Others are clapping their hands. Some fall on the floor in laughter.

"Stop the video! Hurry! I want to watch before the bell rings! Hey! You can't get up; we just killed you!"

They never cease to amaze me. Assassinate Macbeth?

My English class has just finished our unit on *The Tragedy of Macbeth*. To capture a feeling for the rhythm of Shakespeare, we have beat out the meter of Dr. Seuss's *Green Eggs and Ham,* one side of the room trying to out-chant the other. Then we've beat out the rhythm of Shakespeare (or tried to). We have performed modern-day scenarios: someone has only one ticket to the best concert in town, and only you or your best friend can go; two of you are in line for a promotion and your ambitious wife suggests murder to solve the problem (*Shakespeare Set Free*). We have listened to the audiotapes, watched Polanski's version of the movie (screaming in disgust at the witches), and vied for speaking parts. All that's left is the unit test.

After an objective test consisting of multiple choice and true/false questions, I assign the essay part of the exam: Write a five-paragraph essay (with what is left of the ninety minute class) explaining who you think is the tragic character in *The Tragedy of Macbeth* and why. For prewriting, I play the cassette of Vivaldi's "Four Seasons." My vibrant actors slide back in their desks, moan, groan, lope across the room to sharpen a pencil, scratch something out on paper. Safe behind my desk, I grade yesterday's vocabulary quizzes. *What am I doing? What else do I want from them? They have just written scripts, collaborated, revised, related the text to their own lives, performed, and now I want them to complete an objective test and a pre-formatted essay? What greater proof do I need of their understanding?* I am really hiding in shame behind those quizzes. *Prewriting is Vivaldi? What am I thinking?* My personal prewriting techniques usually last for a period of days and include loading the dishwasher, calling my stepmother, walking two miles, cleaning the bathroom, and checking my email. How can someone who not only believes strongly in the power of the written word, but who also is a graduate student of professional writing, make such an assignment? The students are ripe for writing success and what am I doing about it? I quietly move to turn the cassette over in the tape player and slink back to my desk, hoping no one in the room will notice me.

I began my teaching career in 1995 at Campbell High School in Smyrna. Armed with twenty years of experience in the business world and a cum laude degree in English Education, I was ready to roll up my sleeves and get to work. My head was filled with educational philosophies and foggy memories of my high school's culture as I crossed over into the front lines of my classroom. My expectations demanded the rapt attention of all students, who were to gaze at me intently, while I regurgitated my wealth of knowledge—all for their benefit, of course. If any deviation from this behavior was detected, my head would spin as in *The Exorcist*, smoke would curl from my ears, and my eyes would blacken before they shot a death ray upon the perpetrator. By the end of the year, I had slammed my door one too many times, my students thought I was hilarious (not in a good way), and I was exhausted.

Some days, over the next two years, while standing at the front of the room, droning on, I would have a flashback to the time when I was sixteen, in my own high school English classroom, the young girl in the middle row, trying to be as unobtrusive as possible. While I devoured the literature, I was also thinking of how I had to walk to work after school or wondering if I would have the courage to talk to Romeo tomorrow if I passed him in the hall. I was also thinking how comfortable I felt in that room, how my teacher acknowledged and accepted my quietness. I sensed her unspoken respect for me and mine for her increased.

My Own High School Years

I attended Chamblee High School in Atlanta, Georgia, between the years of 1968 and 1972. My English teacher became my professional model for what a teacher should be. She is the person who made me want to be a teacher. Now, when I search my memories, I remember teacher-centered instruction. We read *A Separate Peace* and the next day she told us what those chapters meant. We read *The Scarlet Letter* and the next day she told us what those chapters meant. We read *The Autobiography of Malcolm X* and *Native Son.* I hung on every word she said. Sometimes her interpretation was exactly what I had thought. Other times it wasn't. Although, at the time, the interpretation was acceptable to me, I wonder now if it was acceptable to the other members of the class. I never questioned it.

We had to memorize twenty vocabulary words a week and write a sentence using the words correctly in context. I remember writing a research paper on *The Great Gatsby*. I also remember reading the novel ten years later to understand what I had read. And I remember a "special senior class" where we just read – read – read. That's all we did. I adored my teacher and hung on every word she said. When I was insecure and unsure of my response to a piece of literature, she validated my thinking, or cleared a concept for me, or opened a new avenue of thinking.

Why did I adore every word she said about literature? Because she validated what I thought about the texts. I needed to hear that from her—*she was the teacher, right?* And because I sensed she respected me as a person; she respected everyone in the class. The presentation was not a condescending exposition of information being offered to us. It was a sharing. And she managed the class with a wry sense of humor that kept those out of line, in line.

My 21st-Century Classroom

In my third and fourth years of teaching, I began to see my students as who they were, not who I wanted them to be or who I had been in high school. I also began to see the "me" under all my self-imposed teacher expectations. I was developing my teaching philosophy based on the adolescent and a sense of self. I could see where my responsibility was. I wanted to help my students develop goals and discover the power of their minds. I wanted to help prepare them to become confident, successful, functioning members of society. So how was I going to accomplish that? How was I going to remake my teaching to teach all the students, not just the Leslies?

The answer was given to me as a gift. After three years of teaching, I was encouraged by my undergraduate methods teacher, Dr. Sarah Robbins, to begin thinking about graduate school and the Kennesaw Mountain Writing Project, a National Writing Project site. I became a fellow in the summer of 1998. During that summer I began to visualize how I wanted my classroom to be. With Sarah's and my colleagues' encouragement, my teaching philosophy began to take form, based on three theories of teaching writing.

The first is the theory of community, where the writer is viewed as a member of a group who has common goals and abilities. Each member of the group brings his or her own literacy history to the class. These literacies include family, neighborhood, school, community and ethnic group. My classroom is a community (culture) of its own, composed of all these diverse literacies, and I want each student to take ownership in that culture. The classroom becomes its own community with its own literacy. We begin by writing, illustrating, and sharing our first memories of reading and writing. We develop personal maps that bring us to the present, where we can move forward as one group. The classroom becomes a non-threatening place of learning, a haven.

The second theory that shapes my philosophy is the theory of expressivism. While I believe in the concept of my classroom as one community, I also want each student to feel that he or she is unique. I believe in the use of journal responses and personal narratives to develop a strong sense of self that will carry over into adulthood. Both of these types of writing, while promoting self-discovery, also build confidence in writing, no matter what type of literacy background a student brings to the classroom. Journals and personal narratives can also be the bridge between a student's life and the literature of the curriculum. This bridge engages the student and demonstrates the universality of good literature.

The third theory to shape my teaching philosophy is the traditional classical theory. While the security of a classroom community promotes ownership in learning and expressivism promotes self-discovery and value, without the ability to think critically the student will not be able to function successfully in the adult world. The use of logic and rational thought is a necessary skill, whether one needs to manage a family, to understand the workings of a cash register, or to write a business plan. Developing an argument, determining an audience, researching for evidence and arranging support for that argument in a logical manner develop a thought process that will ensure future success.

I put these theories to work during my fourth year of teaching. We became a community that laughed, cried, and even danced together. Occasionally, when the class's enthusiasm bordered on the rowdy side, I would ask my students if they wanted to see me in my role from *The Exorcist*, but they never did. They just wanted to hear the story of the bad old days when I had demanded all eyes to stare with rigid compliance upon me while my students moved only in the choreographed steps I read from my lesson plans. One reason our classroom culture became successful is that I believe so strongly in the power of community. That passion was transferred to the students, and it became their passion too. So with this environment ripe for collaborating and writing and editing and revising, did we? *Not exactly*. While I was now able to articulate my philosophy of teaching, something was still missing from my belief system. I understood the process of establishing a writing community. I felt strongly the power of the written word. But did I really believe it for my classroom, and did I guide my students to write with an understanding of their own links to a belief system of their own?

I put in a call to Stella Ross. Stella was in charge of the high school language arts curriculum in Cobb County. When I called her, in 911 mode, I was looking for teacher models in the county who have created successful classroom writing communities. Stella immediately recommended four teachers and agreed to help me arrange for professional development time to observe these potential mentors at work. I selected two, based on their teaching settings and demographic similarities to my high school. Stella couldn't have been more intuitive. One teacher exemplifies my philosophy of community and expressivism. The other is a true model of the traditional classical model.

Lisa's Classroom

Three miles down the road from my Campbell High classroom, off Windy Hill Road, Osborne's tardy bell is ringing for Lisa Cherry's second period Honors American Literature class. As the students settle in their seats, Lisa is standing by the front door, paper in hand, and begins to speak as the last bell rings.

"I've got twenty-five questions for review for *The Great Gatsby* test tomorrow. Extra credit for every one you get right. Somebody keep score." Lisa reads the questions and the class calls out the answers. No one is writing them down. Everyone is engaged. "How many points is that now, fifteen? Good. Okay. If you don't get this one you're retarded!" Everyone laughs and Lisa continues to call out questions. "I don't even know this one," Lisa remarks before one question. During the review, Lisa is interrupted once by a knock at the door, which she handles as she continues to fire off questions and field answers. She never breaks her rhythm. She does look back at me and casually remarks, "I get interrupted about sixty times a period."

Lisa moves on to the next assignment. The day before, the students had received a list of writing topics for *The Great Gatsby*. Today their assignment is to write for one hour, from a topic chosen from the list, a five paragraph essay, double-spaced, in rough draft form.

"Everyone settle down. Let's get to work. You've got one hour. You can use the computers at the back of the room if you want." Because Lisa is yearbook sponsor, her students have the benefit of seven computers at the back of the class. Several students move back to the computers, as a girl and a boy settle at Lisa's desk; one girl climbs onto the counter top that lines the outside wall of the room. One boy pulls a stool up to the same counter and writes as he looks out the window at the falling rain.

"Who has questions? I'll help you get started with the first paragraph. Take a book from the shelf if you need it."

Lisa hasn't stopped moving since class began. "Mrs. Cherry, I need your assistance," comes a request from the other side of the room. Several hands are raised and Lisa moves to help them. After talking with several students individually, providing ideas and encouragement for beginning paragraphs, Lisa moves to the first row of students and begins to stop at each desk.

"How are you doing? Let's see what you have here. Good. Why don't you. . . ?" Over the next forty-five minutes, Lisa works her way to each student's desk. "Who haven't I talked with yet?" She keeps moving. Once I hear her say, "that's cool" as she reads a draft.

Students are teasing each other and sharing thoughts; "Hey, what do you think of this line? Where is it in the book where . . . ?"

Lisa then announces, "I'm going to stop taking questions now. I want you to stop talking and write quietly." She comes by my desk and tells me she really does like a quiet classroom when they are writing. "*Really,*" she says.

Students continue to raise their hands and Lisa continues to move to help them. "I've lied. I said I'd stop taking questions." But she doesn't. She is moving and helping, nonstop. "They are not afraid of me," she quips as she goes by my desk.

One student turns around and says to me, "She's so nice." When Lisa positions herself against one counter top, the students come to her.

As the hour ends, students bring her their rough drafts for approval. "Oooh! Listen to this sentence everyone!" Lisa reads aloud a sentence from someone's essay.

"Why don't you read one of my sentences?" someone else calls out.

"Well, bring it here. Let's see what you've got." And so they hover around her like bees on honey until the end of class. "If you're finished with your draft leave it with me, or you can bring it in tomorrow."

Roger's Classroom

"My hand is history; my palm is literature," croons Roger Hines as he begins his lesson on literary criticism. It's fourth block at Oakwood High School, three miles northeast of Osborne, and his audience of eight males and three "diamonds in the rough" listen respectfully. "Three diamonds in the rough, Ms. Walker," Roger reiterates softly. Their composition notebooks are open, ready for note-taking. They have just completed a seven-question quiz on last night's reading of "Dover Beach." Quizzes have been traded, graded, and passed "all the way to the left" for Roger to collect and record.

Roger passes out three pages of handwritten notes on literary criticism and begins his lecture with an example of how texts can be corrupted over time. He begins to sing part of a Sunday school hymn, "At the cross…." His performance is short-lived though, stopped by his own, and the class's, laughter. "Note that the original word 'worm' has been replaced by the word 'sinner.' A prerequisite to criticism is to have authentic text. The text of this hymn is no longer authentic. We have to ask ourselves, what is the authentic text, or the text which the author intended, and how has it been 'corrupted'?"

Roger calls on Joey, the first student in the first row, to read aloud parts one and two of the first page of the handout. Joey, with baseball hat on backwards, takes a brief glance back toward me, where I sit next to Roger's desk, and begins to read confidently. Joey had been a student in my Brit. Lit. class for a period of about two days at the beginning of the school year.

"Thank you, I'd like to hear more from you in a second," nods Roger, as Joey completes his reading. Roger then calls on the second person in the first row, a young girl, to continue reading. The class completes reading the handout in this fashion, with Roger making comments at the end of each section. "I don't want you thinking like me, I just want you thinking." Then he calls on the next person in "line."

"I'm going to take you on a short walk through a dense forest," says Roger. He divides them into four groups, assigns a leader for each group, and asks them to take out their homework questions on "Dover Beach." As a group, they are to check and confirm their answers and identify the line number where they found the answer. The room quietly changes from five neat rows into four neat circles of desks. The students are comfortable yet industrious as they work. Roger moves from group to group, informing each leader that he will be responsible for sharing certain answers with the class. The class works quietly for ten minutes. There is only one interruption, a knock at the door.

Roger graciously opens the door to an administrator who asks if she can briefly poll the class. She wants to make sure they have all received their personal invitations to the upcoming senior breakfast. One student raises his hand and says he doesn't have one. "Greg, we must make sure that you get your invitation," Roger asserts with concern. "Have you checked with your first block teacher? He should have passed them out this morning. Don't worry. We'll make sure we straighten this out."

The administrator leaves with a smile, and Roger, the traditional Southern gentleman, after a reassuring nod to Greg, leads a review of the homework questions, calling on each leader for their answers, then thanking them for their contributions. One girl remarks, "After we talk about the poem I understand it. I didn't when I was reading it last night."

Roger then turns on the overhead, where he has previously written three word pairs, elucidation (facts), interpretation (claims), and evaluation (opinions).

"Who would like to come to the overhead and complete this chart for 'Dover Beach'?" Roger asks. There is a moment of silence. "Now, we are all in this together," Roger coaxes with a smile. "Who would like to give it a try?" Another moment of silence, then Joey raises his hand (*I'm so proud of him*). He moves to the overhead, and slowly completes the chart, as Roger offers suggestions and reassurances. "Good, Joey. Thank you. Now who else would like to try?" A girl volunteers without hesitation and goes confidently to the overhead where the procedure is repeated. Roger offers encouragement as she works.

Roger then asks the students what they thought of their second homework assignment: the reading of "Ah, Are You Digging on My Grave?" by Thomas Hardy. Several students raise their hands to offer their opinions. Comments and opinions are accepted respectfully. He then presents the following examples of optimism and pessimism to be recorded in their composition notebooks:

Optimism	**Pessimism**
Glad	Sad
Positive	Negative
Half full	Half empty
Thorn bushes have roses	Rose bushes have thorns

There are only ten minutes left in the class. Roger asks the students to end the day by writing a journal entry. Because it is the end of the year, he wants the class to reflect on school life and to project where they will be in the next two to three years. Someone asks, "How long does it have to be?"

"Try for at least one page. Just start writing down your thoughts." They write for a few minutes.

"I see we've run out of time. You'll have to complete this for homework. I'll give you a sentence starter—'As the session comes to a close...'"

Summer Learning for the Teacher

The semester came to a close and the year ended. The summer was filled with The Kennesaw Mountain Writing Project's Advanced Writing Institute and a graduate class, Composition Pedagogy for High School and College Teachers. Now I was able to put the names of theorists to my philosophy of education. David Bartholomae sees the writer as a member of a group of writers who have common goals and abilities—a *community*. Peter Elbow views the writer as a unique individual, concerned with self-discovery instead of communicating—*expressivism*. Edward Corbett views the writer as an orator of argument or persuasion, concerned with effective presentation and credibility—*traditional classical*.

My participation in the advanced writing group and the study of past and current theories of composition in the composition pedagogy course helped me see more clearly the strands in Lisa's and Roger's classrooms and what I wanted to take away from them. The experience also showed me that I already had some of those strands in place.

In reflection, I see that, while I didn't believe it at the time, my class had become a writing community. I didn't see a performance of *Macbeth* as a valid, tangible or credible means of measuring understanding. I didn't see it as writing. I see it now. Writing is a tangible, touchable thing. And while it doesn't have to be in the form of a five-paragraph essay, it is a valid means of creating, communicating and assessing. *What more could I have asked for with Macbeth?* I look back and see parts of Lisa's expressive community and parts of Roger's tradition in my classroom. I also see parts of me. Not the me that gazed at my high school English teacher with rapt attention, but the growing me that shares a writing community with my students.

I couldn't wait for the school year to begin.

So it did, and armed with a strengthened belief in the writing community, I faced three classes of ninth graders. Fall semester moved quickly. While respecting the diversity of each student, we had become a community with its own literacy. We had shared literacy histories and responded to literature in personal journals. During one writing assignment in the ninth grade honors class, a five-paragraph essay on a character's development in *The Tragedy of Romeo and Juliet*, I drew upon what I had observed in Lisa's classroom. I moved from student to student, providing assistance, suggestions, and praise. During another assignment, a four-paragraph essay analyzing figures of speech and imagery in "The Raven," I used a more traditional approach: group work assisted by overheads and outlines.

But it wasn't until the end of the semester that I was inspired by a lesson that kept me awake one night as it developed in my mind. I couldn't wait to share a new reading and writing experience I envisioned, inspired by a graduate class I was taking at Kennesaw. I was enrolled in Dr. Sarah Robbins's class, Multicultural Perspectives in Literature. We were reading

The House on Mango Street, Letters from Rifka, Zlata's Diary, and *A Farewell to Manzanar*. Through discussion, writing and technology searches, we were devising ways to teach these texts in our classrooms. I found particular interest in *The House on Mango Street*.

Would this book appeal to one class of twenty-three students, comprised of seven African-Americans, eleven Caucasians (one from Bosnia), four Hispanics, and one Asian living in a transient, urban environment? Can my students relate the writing of Sandra Cisneros to their lives? Can they write about a memory of home? Could they prove to me, through writing, that there is a universality that cuts across all cultures? Can the places where they have lived, and where they live now, reflect the beauty of their lives, not only in imagery and style, but also in their memories? Do I have a strong enough commitment to the power of writing to give this assignment?

I felt strongly that Cisneros's text would build a bridge between the written word and the students in my classroom. Marianna told me every day she was leaving for Mexico (home) and didn't know if she would be back. Mama said she would be. Seventeen-year-old Joey, monitored by his parole officer, succeeded every day in pushing all my buttons until I snapped and sent him out of the room. Rachel sat sweetly and quietly, acquiescing to every demand of my lesson plan. Christi asked every day, "Was I good today, Ms. Walker?" Joel showed up late, on the rare days he came to school, with a tank top and tattoo, slamming the door to announce his entrance and flipping his long hair as he begged to go to the counselor's office. Que squirmed in his seat, uncomfortable in a literature class because he was also in a basic reading and writing class.

My Thursday plan was to read as many vignettes as forty-five minutes allowed and have the students respond to them in a double-entry journal. Patsy Hamby, a colleague in graduate school at Kennesaw had reported success with this strategy, and I thought this would be a non-threatening way to have the students relate the literature to their lives. Prentice Hall's *Writer's Companion: High School* describes this type of journal as "a give-and take-with the literature…that can help you think and feel more deeply about what you are reading" (105).

After reading the first vignette, "The House on Mango Street," I modeled a journal entry on the board:

Quotation	**Response**
windows so small you'd think they were holding their breath	Can windows hold their breath? An example of personification.

That's all I asked of them for forty-five minutes. The first several vignettes were fine, but then things started to change.

"When do we get out of here?"

"Can we turn on some music?"

"This is stupid."

"You can't control your class, Ms. Walker."

"Can I go to the bathroom?"

I was starting to break. With twenty minutes left in the class, Cisneros and I had lost them. I was so excited this morning when I came to school, so excited to share this book with the class, and they hated it. I was really starting to crumble. In fact, I was starting to cry, but I thought, I am going to read to them until the bell rings. I read, and I walked up and down the aisles as I did. It sounds melodramatic now, but I was reading "Darius and the Clouds," and it *really* was making me cry. But I wasn't going to stop. So I read and they listened and they were still and they looked at each other because they thought I was crying. But I didn't. I just kept on reading about the clouds "like pillows" (Cisneros 33), and then they wrote, and then the bell rang.

On Friday I was mad. *What is it about this text that makes you squirmy and antsy and bored? So bored you throw your head back on the desk behind you as you slump in your seat. You can't sit for forty-five minutes and have someone read to you and then write about it?*

"For the next hour, after completing this outline, you are going to write a rough draft, imitating the style of Sandra Cisneros. There is to be no talking, only writing, and I expect 500 words, no less!"

"Five hundred words?"

"Five hundred words is nothing. Look at 250." I showed them the first several paragraphs of Cisneros's first vignette. "This is 250 words."

"You're just mad because of yesterday, Ms. Walker."

God, they're smart. Yes, I was, but it was the anger that gave me the strength to hold on to and go forward with a writing lesson I felt so strongly about. I wasn't backing down. I didn't, and they wrote. I gave the ones that didn't finish the weekend to complete their rough drafts. It was painful to watch as they painstakingly counted every word.

"I've only written 250 words, Ms. Walker."

"That's because you've been sleeping for twenty minutes, Joey. Sit up and keep writing."

He did. They all did, and the results were beautiful. I learned from the experience that Rachel doesn't know what cumulus clouds are. I learned that the main reason some students move is because "the house is falling apart and not worth putting money into," or so a parent says. I learned divorce makes for lots of moves and that David misses California. Christi won't go back to her first house because the memories of her grandmother are too painful. I learned that the loss of a young friendship because of a move hurts.

I believe the resistance I received from the beginning was actually due to a connection with the text my students sensed with the reading of the first vignette. A need for a sense of place is a common value that cuts across all cultures. This connection cut into the culture of my classroom and opened a place that was threatening to move into. It was also threatening to ask my students to write about something personal, when they are used to regurgitating the formulaic three-pronged thesis (painful enough in itself).

Although I was frightened too, the experiences of the previous year—reflecting on my own teaching practices, observing successful teachers of writing in the community, participating in The Advanced Writing Institute, and continuing graduate classes at Kennesaw in the Master of Arts in Professional Writing program—have given me the courage to stick to my convictions to establish a writing community in my classroom. I think I'm making progress. For now, I'm quite reluctant to return the essays to my students. They are too precious.

Reflection

I've read The House on Mango Street *with a number of classes in the years since I first drafted this essay. Fortunately, my classroom's become a more comfortable community: the room is more clearly "our" space instead of just "mine," and, as a result, students are more comfortable and productive as writers. What's different? What have I learned? And how did my writing group and the inquiry community for this project support that learning?*

First of all, I've learned that I have to recognize the particular needs of each class; there is no formula. Just as Andy had to rethink his instructional strategy for the Writing Project site's summer writing groups and Vicki had to rethink hers for the grade school classroom, I have to adapt my strategies each semester. Working with Andy and Vicki provided confirmation of a valuable understanding that had been developing very slowly in my pedagogy: I must constantly rethink, reflect, and refine my teaching of writing. The writing situation is going to be different for each classroom because the dynamics and personality of each classroom is different. And that's okay. In fact, when Andy, Vicki, and I first got together to try to work as a writing group, we found the challenge especially difficult since one thing we were aiming to collaborate on was reflecting on our working processes.

Fortunately, we also found that getting to know each other personally helped our writing group function better. After we spent some time together socially, we could get down to the harder work of collaborating on our pieces. Then, we realized we did have the common bond available to all writers—the challenge of writing itself.

These days, I share that realization with my students.. I have a basic structure in place that includes writing all of the following essays: one personal narrative, one literary analysis, one comparison/contrast paper, and one persuasive essay. I often use The House on Mango Street *as the vehicle for the personal narrative. But one semester it didn't work that way. By the time we got to reading* The House on Mango Street, *it was late in the year, and I didn't see any time available for the essay, so we used the novel as a tool to recognize themes and figurative language. The class had already written a personal artifact essay, so I felt okay leaving the* Mango Street *writing assignment out. Yet in another semester, we not only wrote the* Mango *essay, but after reading the "Hips" vignette about jumping rope, we went outside to emulate the scene. This activity happened in only a single class, because one of the students brought in a jump rope. Watching one 6'5" basketball player unabashedly attempt to double Dutch will remain one of my fondest teaching memories.*

I've also learned over the years that the number of students, time of day, and gender makeup will determine the dynamics and personality of a class. My classes usually average thirty students. If it is first block, they are usually quiet. If it is third, they are hungry, then sleepy. But a leader usually emerges, either someone with strong verbal skills who likes to share his or her writing, or someone with a personality that wins the class over.

The patience and adaptability that I can now take into my classroom came out of my own experience in my writing group. There I learned to be flexible, to open up to the diversity and transience of writing with a group. The benefits continue to spill over into the classroom. And I'm having a lot more fun with my teaching.

I'm also having more fun as a writer. I've had two essays published in professional publications growing out of curriculum development projects sponsored by our National Writing Project site. In "Making the Classroom Our Place," an essay in Writing Our Communities, *I share a lesson I use in ways similar to, yet different from, my past approach of linking a reading of "Darius and the Clouds" to personal writing. I describe how my students now create personal history maps—highly visual texts that would also be at home in Vicki's classroom and that are modeled on the illustrations in the children's book* My Place. *I explain how this activity leads us to a sense of our classroom as a community with many histories, a community that can become "our place" through collaborative reading and writing. In my essay for* Writing America, *I revisit a field trip that built on and generated community research, and I emphasize ways that collaborating with my students enriched my teaching. The confidence to try these teaching experiments came, in large part, from participating in inquiry communities like the one behind this book. And the ability to* **write** *about my experiences grew from the support of writing groups. One important lesson writing groups have taught me is this: I should have confidence in myself because I am a good writer. And I'm much better when I write with colleagues.*

References

Berlin, James. *Rhetoric and Reality: Writing Instruction in American Colleges, 1900-1985.* Carbondale: Southern Illinois UP, 1984.

Cisneros, Sandra. *The House on Mango Street.* New York: Vintage Books, 1989.

Hamby, Patsy. Personal interview. 7 Oct. 1999.

Harris, Joseph. *A Teaching Subject: Composition Since 1966.* Upper Saddle River: Prentice Hall, 1997.

Macbeth. Dir. Roman Polanski. Playboy Productions, Inc. and Columbia Pictures Industries, 1971.

O'Brien, Peggy, ed. *Shakespeare Set Free.* New York: Washington Square Press, 1993.

Paramount Communications Company. *Writer's Companion: High School.* Englewood Cliffs: Prentice Hall, 1995.

Writing Groups Revised: Coaches, Community, and Craft in a Summer Institute

Andy Smith
Pebblebrook High School

As I walk to the gazebo, I hear the frantic scribbling of pen on paper. Across the lawn at one of the picnic tables, Catherine produces her first manuscript to be workshopped. On another part of the lawn, a group congratulates Ted for turning a creative writing prompt from the day before into a beautiful two-page poem. Standing in the middle of all of this, I can feel the energy and creativity. But this spark among summer institute writing groups was not always there.

I have been affiliated with the Kennesaw Mountain Writing Project (KMWP), a National Writing Project (NWP) site, since I attended the summer institute of 1996. From 1999-2001, I returned to the institute as a mentor. We teach the fellows of the summer institute to become a collaborative community, working with a series of professional research and teacher-generated texts to grow as teacher leaders in their respective schools. As a mentor, I supported that process.

In a sense, the teaching team is a sub-community of teacher researchers composed of the site director, institute co-director, and several teacher mentors. Their function is to observe what goes well and capitalize on those strengths while documenting constraints that the group faces and troubleshooting problems. Being a teaching team member for the Kennesaw Mountain Writing Project enables staff to do informal ethnographic studies as they observe a community of educators in the process of presenting, analyzing, discussing, and reflecting upon a variety of texts. Shirley Brice Heath, in her own ethnographic studies, states that it is important that a community respond, "not only from the information in print, but from the group's joint bringing of experience to the text" (197). In effect, the KMWP teaching staff's examination of their practice leads to their refining of and reflection on that practice through written and oral reflective texts. This essay will describe our own evaluation of our program for writing groups at the institute, how we restructured that program, and what we learned about it, through a teacher research project.

Evaluating the Practice

During the fall of 2000, as happens every year, the teaching team of the Writing Project institute met to evaluate the prior summer's institute. We used our own observations and reflections as well as written and oral feedback from the participants to consider changes in the institute curriculum. This feedback includes written responses and evaluations from the fellows, culled from their weekly reflections submitted during the institute and from informal meetings with teacher mentors.

For several years, most of that feedback was focused on the reading groups, which are designed to provide a means to discuss and apply professional literature. Teachers attending the institute were divided into groups by their choice of text and asked to read and analyze it (See http://kmwp.kennesaw.edu). The groups would then present findings about their readings to all of the fellows. The teaching team worked for two summers to develop an improved reading group structure for institute participants. This new structure included protocols on how the group should operate and guided questions to lead them into their initial reading. In the two-year period between 1998 and 1999, we, as a Teaching Team, had observed marked improvement in the fellows' ability to manage their groups and to analyze, assess, and present their texts.

In the fall of 2000, however, after reviewing the fellows' evaluations for that year, we realized that our focus needed to shift to the *writing* component of the institute. Future participants needed to be given a community framework for managing writing groups similar to that being given the reading groups.

If It's Broke, Fix It: The Birth of a New Coaching System

The NWP summer institute writing groups are intended to allow for collegial motivation, support, and feedback for a teacher's writing in a safe and comfortable environment. At our NWP site, for institutes through summer of 2000, the main product of the writing groups was each fellow's anthology piece published at the end of the institute. For many years, this one piece was the focus of the fellow's motivation for participating in the writing groups.

This "one-piece mentality" all changed when the teaching team added a teacher-writer in residence to our institute curriculum. Most afternoons, the fellows met with the writer in residence and worked with different creative writing prompts in order to build a portfolio of writing samples. The writer in residence generated diverse pieces of writing from the participants which became springboards for other writing activities developed during the fellows' writing time and in their writing groups. The fellows loved the opportunity to create different forms of writing, but this successful addition to our program led to another problem. Instead of fellows having only one piece that they were working on, as in previous years, the pattern emerged of the participants juggling numerous pieces and wanting, feedback on most of them.

The problem, we realized, was that we had devoted so much energy to the reading groups that we had failed to see similar issues plaguing our writing groups since our structure was not based in a conceptual framework to accommodate multiple diverse texts all being composed by each fellow at the same time. When we increased the writing expectations, the teaching team soon recognized the participants' inexperience working with a community of writers. What they failed to see was that, in addition to helping with their own revision process, the groups were actually small "classrooms" to acquire tools for teaching writing, revision, and reflection, while bringing their experience to a multitude of texts as envisioned by Heath.

For seasoned writers accustomed to working in groups, bringing their experience to this sub-community seemed easy, but the novices had problems. Therefore, the first meetings of some groups were a mixture of chaos and collegiality. These groups quickly looked to the teaching team for answers: What was the group's organizational structure? How did they handle issues of leadership? What were they supposed to do for an hour when they met? We confronted these issues on a case-by-case basis and began to change the face of the writing groups. Then, in the fall of 2000, the teaching team used teacher research techniques to set some broad goals to improve the writing group experience.

Connecting our analysis of institute evaluations with our own professional reading about writing groups, we revised our use of writing groups. We asked: "How can we structure the groups to create a supportive community as opposed to an unfocused meeting of different participants with different pieces and different goals?" Our objective was to find out how to bring this authentic collaborative practice about.

The answer was really right before our eyes. For years, we had been bringing in past fellows, now teacher consultants, as demonstration coaches. Why not do the same for the writing groups? Thus the writing group coaches, or facilitators, were born. Their role was to help establish a comfortable structure for each individual group to operate under, while modeling approaches for workshopping and revision of multiple pieces of writing in a collaborative environment.

Coaching Writing Coaches Through Research on Revising

We decided to select three coaches, former summer institute fellows, who we hoped could help us meet the main goals of the project; we collaborated with them to plan the activities they would use to help guide new fellows during the institute. We realized that this endeavor would be a great opportunity for our site to conduct a teacher research project. The goal was to study the process of coaching the writing groups while also assessing how well the groups operated under the flexible guidelines established by the coaches. This collaborative research project allowed us to capitalize on a major component in the National Writing Project vision: developing teacher leadership. We would be able to study the impact that a leader has on a community of learners. This study would also allow us to observe the strategies that the leader used to build a collaborative community out of the writing group.

Another key aspect of the research project was reflection. We realized we would have to reflect daily on the practices and products of each writing group and we also realized, as in any teaching situation, the need to analyze and modify the daily curriculum to meet the writing groups' needs. So besides creating a plan to add coaches to enhance our writing groups, we developed a related plan for coaches to study their own teaching strategies.

We sent out a listserv call that detailed our plan and goals and asked for interested volunteers comfortable modeling strategies for writing, workshopping, and revision. From a number of volunteers, we chose three coaches. They were Betsy Bunte, a teacher at Campbell High School; Chris Golden, a middle school instructor at The Walker School; and Vicki Walker, a teacher at Compton Elementary School. These candidates agreed to return for the morning portion of the institute for one week, and Scott Thompson, the teacher co-director of the institute, sent the new coaches a packet of materials to read before our initial meeting date. The fellows would read these selections, as well.

These selections had been chosen from texts about writers and the writing process. Prior fellows had been asked to make recommendations for books that would be helpful in refining our writing groups. After a list was generated, Scott and I reviewed the works and assembled ones that we felt would be beneficial to the coaches and the groups.

When Scott and I held our planning meeting with Betsy, Chris, and Vicki in March, we created objectives focused on supportive reading, key rhetorical concepts to guide writing, and models for revision. It was important to include the coaches in decision making, as they needed to share the same vision for this teaching and research project. After discussing what we felt were essential components for creating a safe and productive writing community, we decided upon the following additional aims for each coach to accomplish with a group:

- review the concepts of voice, tone, and audience;
- distinguish between local and global revision;
- model the writing and revising process for the fellows;
- create group protocols for discussing and revising writing.

With only four meetings to establish their group procedures and protocols, the coaches wanted to keep the readings short, but substantial, so we did not use all of the selections in the original proposed list. The final reading list included an excerpt from Stephen King's *On Writing* that dealt with the different processes that individual writers use in their craft as well as a piece from Lucy Calkins' *The Art of Teaching Writing* on writing notebooks and workshopping. Our final two selections came from Brown, Mittan, and Roen's *The Writer's Toolbox*. These pieces addressed local and global revision.

Steering the Groups

After a May pre-institute workshop for the upcoming participants, the teaching team divided the fellows into their writing groups. In line with the NWP's focus on teaching writing in kindergarten through university, these groups were diverse in experience and level of education taught, comprised of teachers at different levels and comfort zones with their own professional and personal writing. Our concept for forming groups, in other words, is different from that of author Ursula Le Guin. The teaching team had been reviewing sections of her work *Steering the Craft: Exercises and Discussions on Story Writing for the Lone Navigator or the Mutinous Crew*. Le Guin presents a lengthy appendix on how to organize and implement writing groups. We saw these protocols as a good place to start, initially, in our attempts to refine the groups. However, we realized that we had a philosophical difference with the author's view that "a peer group works best if everybody in it is on the same level of accomplishment" (151). Le Guin asserts that some more experienced members may resent having to work with more novice writers. Le Guin also urges a larger group, as opposed to our groups of three or four (151). We thought, though, that the blending of different levels of comfort, experience, and background would produce greater collaboration. A diverse community would bring greater variety of texts and ideas to the group, allowing for individuals to grow as writers and teacher leaders. We anticipated the diversity in the ability levels of their students when these teachers returned to the classroom. For us, the writing groups were to be as much about teaching collaborative revision as about improving individuals' pieces.

Let the Games Begin

In the second week of the Summer Institute, the coaches met daily with their groups to get the groups running. The sessions lasted for one hour each day for four days and included discussion of readings, techniques, and writing strategies. Eventually, the coaches also modeled the workshopping and revision process for the groups.

After their meetings with the groups, the coaches met daily with me to debrief. They would start by filling out a daily reflection and evaluation that assessed each group's grasp of the curriculum (especially strategies for collaborative revision) as well as the comfort level the group had at forming a bond and a community. Once we had completed these reflections, we had a roundtable discussion where the coaches shared their experiences with their group and identified problem areas. At this time we also made changes to the next day's agenda when appropriate. Once the coaches had finished their debriefing, I compiled their information into one daily reflection for documenting and analyzing our research. Based on my field notes and the coaches' reflective daily reports, I will now describe our team's progress through the four-session coaching period.

Day One: The Ideal Reader

At our pre-planning meeting, the coaches had identified the need to establish a trust factor with all of their members, so community building was our goal for the first day. Even though this was the first meeting of the writing groups, the fellows had been meeting as a large institute community for three days prior to the arrival of the facilitators, so the facilitators were the "new kids" and had to assimilate into the groups quickly. This acculturation was accomplished in numerous ways. Most facilitators talked about themselves and then allowed the other members to introduce themselves. Some facilitators even shared stories about how nervous they were with the writing groups at their own summer institutes and talked about their anthology pieces. This was, perhaps, the most critical aspect of the new writing group model. The facilitator had to become a member of that community in order to meet our intended outcomes. The facilitators then asked the group members to set writing goals.

They assured them that these goals did not have to be lofty, just a topic of their choice. Group members had an opportunity to talk about their writing and experiences as writers, as opposed to their experiences as teachers.

The main discussion for the first formal meeting stemmed from King's book *On Writing: A Memoir of the Craft*. King addresses the concept of having an Ideal Reader and suggests that the author keep the Ideal Reader in mind when writing (219). The group discussed the characteristics of an Ideal Reader and considered the feedback the Ideal Reader would give. In essence, the groups were setting the protocols for their own groups. This discussion also established the group's sense of community and comfort.

During the afternoon's debriefing, the coaches gave their initial assessment of the groups. They quickly identified strengths and constraints. Many of these challenges stemmed from the different confidence levels that group members had with writing. Weaknesses included members who inadvertently dominated the conversations. Most coaches agreed that the King piece helped in discerning differences in individual writing styles. We also realized that the coaches might have to take a more active role in pulling all group members into the discussion by asking directed questions to individual members and modeling more formal interaction.

Each writing group had set one initial goal during their first meeting. The majority of groups wanted to bring in one piece that they would be able to workshop by the end of the week. They also wanted to make sure that they had formulated their own protocols for workshopping each other's pieces by this time. This aim mirrored the coaches' initial plan, as well.

Because the groups seemed to be comfortable with one another and recognized their similarities and differences as writers, we moved them into the next stage of our model for a group-supported writing process: establishing voice in their writing.

Day Two: Betty Crocker and the Three Bears

On the second day, Betsy started a session for all of the fellows by reading a passage from Barbara Kingsolver's *The Poisonwood Bible*. She had chosen this piece because of the author's voice, our topic for the day. The passage described the African Congo through the eyes of Leah Price, the daughter of a missionary from Georgia. Upon the family's arrival in Africa, Leah stated, "We came from Bethlehem, Georgia, bearing Betty Crocker cake mixes into the jungle. My sisters and I were all counting on having one birthday apiece during our twelve-month mission. 'And heaven knows,' our mother predicted, 'they won't have Betty Crocker in the Congo'" (13). Betsy used this piece to talk about the concepts of voice and how voice is instrumental in establishing authenticity as a writer. Kingsolver's use of dialect and colloquialisms such as "Lordy" and "plumb let go" illustrated different ways an author can use language to establish a specific voice in a text (22).

The coaches then met with their individual groups and used the "Rehearsal" piece by Calkins to discuss teaching voice in the classroom. Fellows were asked to respond to questions such as "Does keeping a notebook or journal help to establish and recognize voice?" This led into a discussion of Calkins' quote from Thucydides, "Stories happen to those that tell them" (27). We discussed the multiple ways that we tell stories both in oral and written form. The coaches then pulled the discussion around to the fact that to tell a story authentically, an author must have a sense of voice that fits the story. We then discussed ways of finding our own voice as authors and how to make connections between our own writing practices and those we model in the classroom.

One exercise asked the fellows to do a quick-write version of "Goldilocks and the Three Bears" in a voice different from their own. Fellows had an array of selections to choose from, such as pop stars and literary characters. After the writing time, everyone read his or her piece to the group. This was the first time that we asked them to share with their group, and each facilitator gauged the comfort level of the groups. Since the assignment was humorous, all group members felt comfortable sharing and enjoyed the exercise.

The exercise was also important in drawing out the various voices within each group. The coaches asked the group members to tell why they had chosen to write in that particular voice. We also looked at vocabulary and jargon associated with each voice that made it authentic and unique. Some groups then discussed the various voices that they use in their writing. One technique that emerged in some groups was to discuss the variety of voices that the members use everyday, such as "teacher voice" and "parent voice" and to elaborate on the differences in style and syntax associated with those voices.

During the debriefing session, the coaches agreed that the "Goldilocks" prompt helped to ease the tension of reading an original work out loud in the group setting, creating bonding in the community. The coaches then encouraged the group members to bring in some of their own original works that they could use as a model piece for the next day's work: revision.

Day Three: Global Revision and Local Communities

On day three, the coaches met with their groups to discuss a somewhat uncomfortable topic: the concept of revision, both local and global. Many of the fellows shared their students' angst about looking at a piece of their writing and changing it. The coaches began by explaining the difference between changing and revising. One produces a different product, the other a stronger product.

In shifting the focus from the participants' own work, the coaches asked the groups to think about the kind of revision techniques students use in their classroom and to identify them as "local" or "global" (terms in the chapter entitled "Global Revision" from Brown, Mittan, and Roen's *The Writer's Toolbox*). After discussing the various ways to integrate the concepts of local and global revision into their students' writing, the fellows were then asked about their own revising strategies. Did they use local or global revision? Did they have an Ideal Reader already? If so, did the Ideal Reader make local or global comments about the piece?

The participants shared with their coaches that, for the most part when reading a peer's work, they only focused on global revision, hoping to satisfy areas of content and style, before becoming more specific with local revisions. Most of this global revision was accomplished by having an Ideal Reader who made verbal or written comments to clarify situations in the writing or identify holes.

Some of the group members felt inadequate to the task of integrating feedback. The coaches posited the idea of writing three to four main questions at the top of the piece that they wanted answered by their Ideal Reader. This strategy would allow members to receive authentic feedback that would be productive for revising and strengthening their work.

Most of the groups had at least one member who allowed the whole group to look at a piece. The coaches modeled workshopping and revision strategies, such as telling first what they liked about the piece. The group members were then able to respond more directly to the questions identified by the author.

During the debriefing, the coaches agreed that all of the participants were highly sensitive to upsetting the author of a piece during workshopping, but were easily able to use the model established by the coaches to create a comfortable, productive, and empowering moment for the authors. The coaches felt that the communities had been moved to their final goal of constructively workshopping at least one piece from each member of the group the next day.

Day Four: Coaches' Advice

On the last day with the fellows, the coaches asked each member to share one piece that was still in the working or rehearsal stage. Members were then asked to workshop the piece for global revisions. This step allowed for the groups to practice protocols learned over the previous three days and to practice critiquing each other's work. The coach, on numerous occasions, modeled different strategies for workshopping and reviewing, allowing for a greater comfort level among group members who may have had varying degrees of experience in a writing group setting. But coaches would also sit back and observe how well the protocols were working.

The coaches had made every effort to ensure that each group was ready to work independently. All of the coaches felt confident about leaving their groups but did leave behind some basic procedures for daily meetings. This advice included such pointers as having a permanent meeting place, making multiple copies of drafts before the meetings, and giving the writing group questions to answer about drafts.

During the last debriefing session, the facilitators indicated they felt that the time spent on the project was positive and powerful. The groups had definite direction and purpose for their writing. The coaches had helped to establish a process and comfort level with the participants' writing. Finally, the coaches felt that this initiative was so productive that we should consider bringing in coaches every year.

What the Research Tells Us

The writing groups are a meaningful component of the summer institute in that they allow the fellows to make connections between their own written works, works of the other members of the writing group, and works from published researchers in the field of education. By giving these groups the proper direction through modeling writing, establishing protocols, and workshopping various pieces, our new coaches had given the fellows the opportunity to work in a fine-tuned, structured community that nurtured those connections with the texts.

In evaluating the success of the program, the teaching team examined the reflections of both the coaches and the fellows. For the coaches the experience was a positive one on many levels. They felt that it was important for members of previous institutes to come back and connect with the new fellows. The coaches even realized how their work with the writing groups would directly affect their own teaching. Vicki Walker said that her experience made her feel as if she would be a better facilitator of her small groups in her elementary classroom. She also realized that with a little direction, it is all right for the students to take the lead in those groups. Other comments suggested the coaches had come to see the importance of time management for individualized groups. The coaches also remarked that group dynamics helped them gauge whether their facilitation of the groups was smooth and productive.

One of the coaches' suggestions was that they should be able to spend at least a full day with the group in order to get to know them better while also observing the concepts that the group members were learning in their afternoon sessions. The coaches felt that this would help them in revising and supplementing the curriculum and objectives for their group. After reviewing this suggestion, the teaching team decided to go a step further by having the coaches attend all day every day for one week during future institutes. This change has allowed the coaches to work with both the writing and reading groups.

For the fellows, the experience was positive in that the coaches gave them a framework to participate in while also helping the members to forge a community of writers, teachers, and teacher researchers. The written evaluations by the fellows at the end of the institute indicated they felt that the writing groups were one of the best aspects of the summer institute because they were able to generate, workshop, and revise multiple texts in an empowering environment. Many fellows indicated that they wanted to continue to meet with their writing groups after the institute ended in June.

For the institute, we learned how to implement a systematic strategy to improve our teaching practice. We had truly revised our writing groups in two different ways. We had literally changed the way the writing groups were structured and run, but we had also seen the purpose and the product of the writing groups in a different light. Through our ongoing reflection on this teacher research project, we will continue to build our program. Our writing groups hum with energy and creativity as never before. We had increased the wattage, so to speak. Like the typical writer, we have realized that a stronger product and a brighter spark come about by constant revision.

Reflection

This piece has gone through many different phases, and I've had the benefit of input from a different writing group at every stage. Looking back, I can see that the support provided by each writing group was tailored to my stage of composing and reflecting at the time. Revisiting the varying kinds of feedback I received has helped me understand how writing groups can be tailored to a variety of circumstances, but also how every approach to collegial support in writing groups can help me grow as a writer and teacher.

The essay actually began as an internship report that I worked on after serving as coordinator of writing groups at a National Writing Project summer institute. During that institute, I was collaborating with several teacher consultants whose job was to help acclimate our new summer fellows to writing groups. At afternoon meetings of these writing group facilitators, we discussed how the activities of groups had gone earlier in the day. Since I knew I would be writing an internship report, I involved these colleagues in my initial brainstorming. Listening to their comments, I was able to gain insight into the individual strengths and weaknesses of each institute writing group. The information that we shared each day affected the work we did for the next day, while also shaping the content of my internship report. The changes we decided to make in our approaches for mentoring the writing groups became the core content of my writing. I found that instead of simply documenting the instructional activities we implemented and our results from those lessons, my report became more reflective, paying attention to the process behind our work and to its implications.

A year after completing the report, I had the opportunity to join the Advanced Institute of the Kennesaw Mountain Writing Project, a small seminar for teachers who wanted to write about teaching. At this point, I gained a new writing group, one whose members had not been on hand in the first summer when I was first working with basic institute writing groups. This writing group helped me expand and re-organize my piece, moving it from a narrative of my initial observations on the internship by re-framing it around some concepts that are important to all NWP institutes. I had sensed the basics of what I wanted to say all along, but having the small group interaction of other teacher-writers at the Advanced Institute and listening to their discussions about my piece really helped me to structure and shape it. I did not have much experience with academic writing, so I struggled trying to reshape my earlier description of my internship into a more analytical report that might be helpful to other institute leaders. Finally, one of my peers at the Advanced Institute recognized that there was a nugget of argument embedded in my narrative. That's when I had my first real "ah-ha" moment. As my work with the piece and the group progressed, I realized that it was through constant oral, shared revision of my work that I was able to see the relevance of what I had done at the institute the previous summer. I had become a teacher researcher! I had become a writer of teacher research!

I also realized, from my own initially tentative efforts with that summer's writing group, why many of my students do not see themselves as writers or do not have much confidence in what they write. Confidence comes from colleagues, I now understood. So I used the revision processes that I had done with the Kennesaw Mountain Writing Project seminar to change my approach to these students. I instituted protocols for writing reflection and social revision in my classroom. I began to implement a peer tutoring and revision process. More importantly, I began to have my students share their work aloud and let them receive positive reinforcement in the form of comments and praise from the whole group. My students began to take pride in their own writing. My students had become writers! And just as I had benefited from the conversations with my writing group, so did they grow when working with their peers.

In the autumn after I had first expanded my internship report during the Advanced Institute, my friend George Seaman assembled a larger team of teachers to study writing groups in action for a different, larger audience. All of us wondered if working in writing groups that were connected to a larger community of practice might support our efforts to refine some of our writing about teaching into publishable form. Most of us had done presentations for audiences in workshops, but had never seen our professional writing in print. We hoped that a broader collaboration, connecting our inquiry to others' research on reflection and teachers' personal growth, could take us to a "next level" of professionalization. So at this point, I brought my narrative into a new writing group of different colleagues—Leslie Walker and Vicki Walker—who knew about NWP summer programs but who had not yet read about my action research project. Leslie and Vicki brought essays they had begun at different seminars for teacher-authors than the one I had attended. We all brought fresh eyes to each other's writing.

Working within my new writing group helped to change the text once again. Leslie and Vicki proved to be invaluable as an audience. They gave me insight as to what needed to be revised or "fleshed out" so that writing teachers at any grade level would find the paper both compelling and easy to comprehend. Perhaps most important, these colleagues helped me see that I needed to clarify the concepts driving the thinking behind the original experiment to revise institute writing groups. We talked together about the principles of social literacy behind the evolution of the institute writing groups, and this process gradually led my essay beyond a narrative account to an interpretive one. Also, since both Vicki and Leslie had done more formal research than I had, they were able to suggest secondary sources for the work as well. Overall, at this stage in my writing, this writing group helped me position my work more clearly within a framework of inquiry and research.

This writing group also taught me crucial lessons about ownership. As a type-A personality, I sometimes have difficulty sharing ownership of my work—including my writing. In this case, I was already so vested in the piece that it was difficult to accept new respondents' suggestions at first, but they critiqued my work in such a positive fashion that I was able to open my eyes to collaboration, which eventually led to validation.

Meanwhile, at the basic summer institutes for the Kennesaw Mountain Writing Project, the venue where I had first started my research into writing groups' potential, the teaching team has continued to refine practices for facilitating writing groups among the teacher participants. We have realized that the same procedures we used for one year may not be relevant at each year's institute. We've *also come to see that different groups attending the same institute may have different needs, so we encourage each group to design its own protocols. This principle applies in my own classroom as well. As educators, we feel more comfortable with a set plan, knowing the process that we want to teach and knowing the desired outcomes for our students. A good teacher and teacher researcher realizes, however, that every plan must be refined according to a particular student group and the author's needs at each stage of composing.*

The parallel to my work in my third writing group has become clear to me. In looking back upon that "final" stage in the development of my essay, preparing my piece for an audience beyond our own National Writing Project site community, I realized the importance that social reflection can play in teaching as well as writing. I had always tried to be reflective about my teaching. But I have come to appreciate the need for placing that reflection within a larger social framework, including scholarship and best practices by other teachers. From that realization, I have developed a need to read more professional literature and seek out staff development for learning new methods of differentiated instruction. Acquiring that mindset made it possible for me to progress from working as instructional lead teacher at one high school to my current job as staff development coordinator for a school district, where I continue to revise my approaches to inservice so as to reach more learning styles. For teachers in my district, I am striving to create a safe, collaborative environment that is conducive to learning and that helps students and teachers excel. The growth I achieved through my own participation in three different writing groups is helping me lead other teachers to these key words for professional learning: revise, refine, reflect.

References

Brown, Stuart C., Robert K. Mittan, and Duane H. Roen. *The Writer's Toolbox*. Boston: Allyn and Bacon, 1996.

Calkins, Lucy McCormick. *The Art of Teaching Writing*. Portsmouth: Heinemann, 1986.

Heath, Shirley Brice. *Ways with Words: Language, Life, and Work in Communities and Classrooms*. Cambridge: Cambridge UP, 1983.

King, Stephen. *On Writing: A Memoir of the Craft*. New York: Scribner, 2000.

Kingsolver, Barbara. *The Poisonwood Bible*. New York: Harper Collins, 1998.

Le Guin, Ursula. *Steering the Craft: Exercises and Discussions on Story Writing for the Lone Navigator or the Mutinous Crew*. Portland: Eighth Mountain Press, 1998.

Part IV

❦

Re-viewing Writing Groups at Work

In the three pieces for this section, we show how our writing groups' work can be situated within larger frameworks for professionalization. First, in "Reading Across Writing Groups," we share examples of project participants responding to drafts being written by colleagues who were not in their own writing groups, but who were part of the community of practice supporting all of us. Second, in "Writing with Our Eyes Open," we offer reports from a team of "first public readers"—a group of educators affiliated with our National Writing Project site whom we invited to review an early draft of our book manuscript. Third, we provide a retrospective narrative on the stages through which our overarching inquiry into writing groups and communities of practice progressed; we position our experiences within a context of scholarship on writing to learn and on successful communities of practice; and we make some recommendations to teachers who want to build on our work.

Reading Across Writing Groups

Linda Stewart, Renee Kaplan, and Deborah Kramb

In "Reading Across Writing Groups," we provide examples of written responses produced when members of our community of practice first began to read drafts being prepared by writers working in groups other than their own.

This was an important step in building our confidence as writers. We were moving from the still-relatively-private, safe space of our writing groups to a more public arena, with a reader who was encountering our written text for the first time—but who knew something about our working process, since that reader was part of our larger community of practice. Significantly, during this draft-swapping stage, readers tended to respond to our texts in part by describing their own perspective on our topic, asking questions that may not have emerged in our writing groups, and using their reading to revisit their own essays' content. This cross-group reading helped us situate our thinking in a broader context, encouraging us to recognize our essays as more than stories of personal experience. After receiving this round of feedback, we discussed the responses in our writing groups and used them to guide additional revision.

The examples below, when read alongside the published essays, show some of the ways our community of practice was shaping work in the smaller, more intimate writing groups. (See also discussion of this exchange-drafts phase in the introduction to Part II, where Renee Kaplan, Sarah Robbins, and Linda Stewart describe trading responses with Vicki and Deborah.)

Linda Stewart's Response to Vicki Walker's Draft

Vicki,

Because I'm not sure whether I'm to be reflecting on my own practices after reading your piece or providing feedback to you, I am attempting to do both.

Reading your essay about collaborating with your colleague Ann to explore how to developing children's writing abilities through images recalls the experiences Sarah and I had as we worked together to accomplish the same thing at the university level. While we may be teaching different ages, there are many commonalities in our approaches. The evolution of your understanding your practices and how they intersect with theory that became apparent through your discussions with Ann are similar to our experience. Your introduction and development of both how to read images for content and then for "authorial technique" (or artistic style) parallels our use of film clips to illustrate content and theme. The shift you note from teacher-centered to student-centered authority as students gain confidence corresponds to our classrooms. Also, keeping writing at the heart of your practice is consistent in your work and ours. (I'm also realizing as I write this that I can't talk about "my" classroom, but "our" classroom—as if Sarah and I were somehow in the same room!)

One of your practices as you developed your "narrative-making program" through wordless books that shouldn't be overlooked is the importance of talk—between you and Ann and among the students as you conferenced with them. Tom Newkirk and Peter Elbow both emphasize the importance of talk (as do many other educators) in the classroom, and your essay reminded me of that research.

I wondered, when I read your realization that students "had a sense of oral narrative structure mastery that was ahead of what they could produce in print," if that intersected with child development theories (e.g. Piaget). I haven't read many of those texts in so long, that I don't remember. But what strikes me after reading your essay, is how talking through the pictures, or "storying" pictures is such a central component of bridging the gap between image and text, whether the students are eight or eighteen. Fascinating insight. I will try to incorporate that strategy more consciously in my own classroom.

Similar to your work, I used the textbook *Seeing and Writing* for several semesters in my composition class that fuses with your intent to use "wordless books to drive instruction." Your essay reminded me of two essays in that text: 1) John Berger's first essay in his book *Ways of Seeing* that states, "seeing comes before words"; and 2) Scott McCloud's "Show and Tell" which is the 6th chapter in *Understanding Comics*. Perhaps comic frames are too sophisticated for elementary school, but I wondered about their uses in your class.

I loved seeing into your class a bit—the description of you sitting at the first grade table; the student's comment, "we 'did' that one yesterday," or how one student internalized your instruction, adding "Pizza Delivery" to the image—all made your experience very immediate and intimate to this reader. I also appreciated how you laid out your plan: 1) build on their skills; 2) use literature as a model; 3) extend their writing abilities. That approach works well at any level for any type of assignment.

I found myself wanting more details about specific student's work and how they successfully moved from the visual to the verbal. You mentioned how you worked with them to develop details for their tripartite narratives, and I was eager to hear how they did so. You were honest about how some students weren't developmentally ready for this type of sophisticated instruction, but how you patiently nudged them along. I've certainly had this same experience, and when I'm enthusiastic about a particular approach, I have to remind myself that while some students leap into the process, others chug along.

When you talk about moving from reading (images) to writing (with images and text) you discuss techniques. I wondered if you were referring to what you called "authoring techniques" and if you define that as both artistic and writerly? I also quibbled with the notion that "all stories have a beginning, middle, and end." Because we're trying to validate diverse student backgrounds and the ways they tell stories, the triptych model isn't necessarily valid for "all" stories. Maybe "most" would be better. To explain, one of my Korean students told a story of her mother washing clothes with the pebbles in a stream near her home. The story was heavy on description, but there was no moral, no beginning, middle or end. Of all the stories told in the class that day, hers was the one that provoked the most interest and admiration among her classmates. It was a good lesson for me that different cultures have different ways of telling stories. In fact, as I write this now, I wonder—are there wordless books for children using Chinese or Japanese or Vietnamese symbols or images?

As you can see—reading your essay has not only raised awareness of how sound teaching practices work from first grade to grad school, but has given me several angles to explore in my work with visual literacy and its connection to writing. Thanks, Vicki, for the opportunity to read your work.

~Linda Stewart

Excerpts from Renee's Response to Deborah Kramb's Draft

I was eager to read your essay on balancing real life day-to-day situations of teaching, studying, and family. I, too, feel the crunch of time to complete all my projects, and I was hoping to find a cure for dealing with all my "extra" endeavors. The cure wasn't there, but your essay gave me hope from a professional colleague. I am hoping to pursue National Board Certification myself, so there is another tantalizer to this essay for me. Even though you teach first grade and I am in middle school, I will re-read your essay throughout my own journey for National Board Certification.

First, as I began to read your introduction, I thought about the process of our teacher inquiry community. The essay clearly shows the importance of teacher professional identity and working with a cohort group....

Moreover, I was immediately captivated with the strong opening—a grandmother comparing life to a juggling act with four balls: work, family, integrity, and health. As I read your topic and sub-topics, I was excited because I saw the essay was going to be written as a play. I cheered, "What an innovative idea." Then I realized that the essay is divided into three acts, as though you are relating your struggles and triumphs as a teacher to your audience. I could actually visualize you sitting on a stool in the middle of a stage and telling your story to other educators....

Here are some points in the essay where I was thinking and questioning. Some of your reflections are especially helpful as I re-visit my own project. They will help me revise.

"Ironically, teaching is a learning process. I don't believe a good teacher is ever finished learning." Yes, teachers are lifelong learners in teaming, sharing achievements of students and with students, reading the latest research in professional journals, attending conferences, and creating and implementing programs to improve student learning.

"I believe all students can learn and it is my challenge to find the key to teaching them....I make goals for individuals, based upon the goals of the grade level, but not restricted by them." You give examples to support your premise, and I want to adapt this approach in my own middle school classroom [and in writing about it].

"Now my students and I learn together." I see the ... sound teaching principle [and how] my own essay focuses on students and myself learning together....

I admire you for sharing your passion for teaching and your recent past challenges with the rest of us. You note that sharing lessons is not enough, but sharing written reflections and the analysis of successes and failures will encourage others to take risks in their own paths for professional development....

Your juggling act worked for you, but it appears to be a change of balance and sometimes one of the four balls is heavier for awhile, and the other three must equal it in weight. I do not know if all four are ever going to be equally balanced. I presume the key is to empower oneself to stabilize areas of management during extreme shifts in differentiation?

Your essay is encouraging and [shows] a teacher's struggle for professional growth through...written reflection and working with cohorts in both small and large groups.

Deborah Kramb's Response to Renee Kaplan's Draft

When Renee [started to give] a synopsis of her essay [at an inquiry community meeting], I only half listened. Renee teaches eighth-grade gifted students and I teach first grade students and her subject was a study of Holocaust survivors. It didn't occur to me that we would have anything in common other than teachers struggling to teach children how to write. I totally enjoyed reading Renee's essay, however. I found myself reading it at several different levels simultaneously: as a teacher sympathizing with her struggle through a difficult challenge, as an eighth grade student sitting in her classroom and as a friend, pulling for her to be successful and amazed that she would try something so complex. I read the essay as I would a good work of fiction, impatiently moving quickly to find out what happened!

Reading the essay as a teacher, I looked for evidence of good instruction that I might emulate. When Renee reflected on looking at the student's work with questions—saying: "I asked myself if the prompts called for students to construct knowledge,"—I imagined how I could use prompts in my own teaching of writing. When she spoke of adjusting assignments for individual interests, I applauded her.... And, I was so impressed that her reflections helped her focus her objectives when the project started to grow beyond her expectations. That was a lesson I would remember!

But, I kept slipping back into my past self, as an eighth grader faced with a teacher who suggested such a project. How would I have felt? As soon as I read the students reflections I became one of them. Yes, I would be reluctant. As an eighth grader, or even now, would I feel comfortable approaching the subject? I grew along with the students as Renee quoted their reflections. I tried to imagine how they felt about the fact their teacher was modeling journaling and expressing her doubts and confusion. (Did she edit what she read to the students, I wonder?) I suffered along with the students when the project became too big to be finished in a year. I understood completely their conflicting feelings.

And then I became Renee's friend—rationalizing that the students would learn a good life lesson. If something is to be very good it takes time and a lot of effort. I identified and sympathized with her when the students didn't always react as she had assumed they would. She had taken such a big risk! But, I knew she wouldn't give up either—and I could hear her struggle in her journal writings as she mulled over what to do to help the reluctant students or faced the challenge of doing things she had never done before. I knew how uncomfortable she felt. I've been there. I could identify. I cheered her on, hoping there would be a way around the problems, but I also worried that she had taken on too much—and that her high expectations would not be met. More than once I asked myself if I would have taken on such a challenge.

Renee and I both have the experience of the Writing Project behind us and I think that influence acted as a safety net for both of us.... We have struggled with our own writing in the program, supported by our summer institute writing group—and the groups for this project.... Because of her experience, she shared her perceived failures as well as her hopes, without hesitation, or concern about what her readers thought of her. As mine did for me, her writing group gave her positive feedback and restored her confidence. I am sure they acted as a sounding board for her ideas, helping her to clarify her goals because that is what the small writing groups are best at!

When Renee [recently] shared her project and essay with our community of practice, she spoke with confidence and clarity. I could hear her working out details of the essay as she spoke. In describing the details to us, in working to help us understand, she kept herself on track. In the safe environment of the inquiry community she could express her thoughts, and our questions guided the course of her essay. Our interest in the subject reflected the audience she was writing for. As a group we reveled in her struggle and in her successes. We learned from her mistakes and her sharing of them. We are all winners....

The closing [reflection] expressed the support that the writing group gave...to the development of the essay and even [to] the lessons in the unit.... Personally I think the essay was captivating because of...including Renee's and the students' reflections. It is interesting that the fact of writing an essay that could be published would affect the assignments for the students! (Good or not?)

She stated some broad information that would help another teacher in planning a similar unit.... I was impressed that her sharing her own writing enabled the students to move into honest journaling themselves. This also happened in my small writing group among the adults. My reluctance to go out on a limb was overcome with matter-of-fact modeling by other members of the group. I too realize now how important teaming of colleagues is and how motivating support and praise can be. I know that will be in my mind as I face my next class of students.

Writing With Our Eyes Open:
A Collaborative Response to
Teachers' Writing Groups

Zsa Boykin, Toby Emert, Sandra Grant, and Scott Smoot

Establishing a Process for Responding

We have a confession to make. When we first received the editors' invitation to "respond" to the manuscript of this book, we did not envision ourselves as contributing authors. We teachers took "responding" to mean "editing" and "encouraging." We thought we would be, like you, readers on the outside looking in on others' writing, offering our observations and our critiques. What we discovered, however, is that we could participate in the colloquy that is this book. Our purpose in this chapter is to draw you in, too.

The four of us had never worked closely prior to our first coffee-and-donuts meeting in the Writing Center at Kennesaw State University. Sandra, Zsa, and Scott had met at National Writing Project workshops; Toby was new to the others. We had gotten to know each other a little better through e-mail correspondence, where we shared unfiltered responses to the manuscript of this book. Those tentative first reactions via e-mail were a good icebreaker at our first meeting, because we all had questions about each other's responses.

As we explained our observations, we discovered that we had each reacted according to our different roles in education. Sandra told how the book resonated with her experiences of studying educational leadership. Zsa prefaced one of her comments by saying that she read as a parent as well as a teacher. Scott found encouragement in these essays for his interest in publishing teacher research essays. Toby looked at the book for its use in instructing the undergraduate education majors in his classroom. When someone said that this book seemed to address multiple constituencies in the field of education, Scott wondered aloud if we might write responses as personal letters, each addressed to one of those constituencies. We decided to try the idea.

Though we wrote separate letters, we still collaborated. Thanks to the internet, we could post drafts on an electronic bulletin board and read each others' responses on e-mail. In our next face-to-face meeting at a book store coffee shop, we asked each other for clarifications, and we heard our own ideas said back to us, sometimes more succinctly. We began to establish our own mini-community of writers, thus joining the inquiry community of this book. Forming a writing group was as easy, informal, and enjoyable as that. We became part of this book, not just in the sense of adding a chapter, but in the sense of trying out the process it models.

Now it's your turn. Read each of the letters that follow. Whatever your role in education, you will likely find entry for yourself to this continuing conversation, becoming a part of this book as we did.

An Open Letter to Classroom Teachers from Scott Smoot, Middle School Teacher and Published Teacher Author

Dear Classroom Teachers:

You know at least one story from your classroom that could change lives. Teachers across America need to hear it. Still, like me, you hesitate to write it. You dread the research to validate your idea, or you prefer to use your creative energy for your students, or you fear rejection. This book has a message for us: begin now to write; it's less daunting and more urgent than you think. You won't find that message in any one chapter; it emerges in the story behind every chapter.

The real starting point for every essay here was a single question: How can I better serve my students? Other questions follow, as different teacher-researchers wonder "what if?" or worry "how come?" Just asking moves us toward the answer. I know, because twenty years ago, a professor of mine laid aside his syllabus and asked me instead to consider the three hardest problems I still faced in my own classroom after four years' teaching. My proposing solutions to my own problems was his only assignment. He and his library were resources open to me for ideas, but experience and imagination supplied the bulk of my answers. Those three essays I wrote then had immediate impact on my teaching, and they have informed my teaching ever since.

In the authors' reflections that frame each essay in this book, we're reminded how these teacher-researchers pushed themselves and each other beyond easy answers. Leslie Walker describes her classroom where students are engaged and "getting it." We expect the rest of the essay to tell us how to recreate her success. Instead, she asks more critical questions, then visits colleagues' classrooms to view their very different approaches. She reforms her own teaching. But Leslie is a teacher of such integrity and persistence that even good results are again open to question. Her dialogue with colleagues helps her to draw conclusions from painful failures. Some of that dialogue happens in the text of her essay, but it also happens outside the text, in her writing group. We, too, can find friendly insight and encouragement in writing groups.

Besides what writing can do for you and your classroom, there's the potential for teacher writing groups to break the grip of dumb inertia in our schools and systems. *I'm thinking not of the impact of writing on those who read it, but the impact on those who do the writing.* This isn't your usual kind of writing about your own school. I'm used to reporting on what my school does, and I'm used to hearing questions posed—then answered—from a podium. I'd like to see what happens when colleagues set out in small cooperative groups to find answers to the questions "what if," "how come," and "how can we better serve our students?" When they push each other past the easy answers, will change be effected in their classrooms? Will their results leaven the entire building?

Let us practice what we preach, and write to learn.

Yours,

W. Scott Smoot
Middle School Teacher
The Walker School
Marietta, Georgia

An Open Letter to School Administrators from Sandra Grant, Teacher, Former Executive, and Former Administrator

Dear Principals and Inservice Coordinators:

Educational leaders are constantly aware of the fact that communication is the sound and logical foundation on which to build success. As a member of the business sector for many years, I strongly believe that one of the key components of effective leadership is communication through mentoring. The most vibrant use of this book for me personally would be as a mentoring tool. Mentoring can be beneficial to the principal as well as to the teacher. Mentoring can be multi-faceted. We can use it as an evaluative tool; as problem solving for teachers and for the school; and for gaining affirmation for teachers as they work together in writing groups.

Being instructional leaders who have a strong emphasis on student achievement, we can clearly see the need to give the teachers under our tutelage more time to reflect on their specialty. By using the collaborative writing group model, we will find that improvement comes through sharing, reflecting, and writing. A teacher's performance as we see it in a forty-five minute observation may not give the true picture of what that teacher is truly capable of accomplishing. After observing our teachers in the classroom, we should allow them to spend time reflecting on the lesson and writing down their thoughts on how their teaching of this particular lesson affected their students. We could take this even further by allowing teachers at our schools approximately four to eight weeks to form writing groups to talk and get feedback on their written evaluation piece. Teachers could work together in writing groups towards a solution that would improve teaching and learning in the classroom.

Even with budget constraints and high stakes testing looming before us, we can all benefit from this type of participative alliance. We should allow our teachers time to work together in writing groups to achieve a higher level of performance and empowerment. There may be a litany of reasons why there would be "no time" for this type of professionalization. However, we can and should be creative in providing writing group opportunities for our teachers during pre-planning, teacher workdays, post-planning, and even teacher retreats.

Teachers relish support, respect, and cooperation. Using this book, teachers can create their own lessons to learn, strategies to borrow, and plans to improve teaching. The overriding hope of all participants in this book is the desire that their students should benefit from similar opportunities. Communication and trust became the key ingredient for the success of each writing group in this project. Suffice it to say that their determination to have open and honest communication about their essays is carrying over now in the authors' teaching. Administrators cannot effectively mentor every teacher in our schools, one-on-one. Writing groups can allow us to delegate some of our mentoring responsibilities to groups by allowing them to in effect become mentors for each other. As we mentor our teachers through writing groups, we can build communities of unreserved honesty and sincere expression.

Sincerely,

Sandra M. Grant
Educational Leader

An Open Letter to Parents and Student Advocates from Zsa Boykin, Middle School Teacher and Parent of Elementary Students

Dear Parents and Student Advocates:

As a veteran teacher I invite you to step inside the minds of the educators whose classrooms appear in this book. You will have an opportunity to experience intriguing lessons and also to develop an appreciation for teachers valuing the art of reflection as a necessary tool of their profession.

Parents, try this: at the next parent/teacher conference, casually ask your child's teacher if the process of reflecting is a part of his or her lesson preparation. As a parent myself, I have occasionally stood in the kitchen interrogating my daughter with questions such as, "*Why* does the teacher want you to do this? *How* does this homework relate to the content you are learning?" Though I really didn't expect my six-year-old to answer me, I'd like to have the courage to ask her teacher about the literacy development principle behind certain assignments. Go ahead and share my story. Use me as an example. When your child's teacher invites you to ask questions, say, "I have a friend who forever helps her daughter with cute, but nonsensical homework assignments. Contrary to that scenario, I want my child *engaged in learning* even when he or she has fun completing non-traditional assignments. So, could you share with me how you value the art of reflection as a necessary tool for creating and modifying exemplary lessons in your subject area? And how do you teach children to reflect?"

Let's take reflection to yet another level. Some teachers do write about and discuss their classroom experiences with their colleagues. As other professionals, such as doctors, attorneys, and even athletic coaches have benefited from collegial collaboration, these teachers have joined the league of practitioners aiming to solve mysteries, uncover facts, and create strategies that will optimize their students' learning. Teachers' writing groups promote this kind of collaboration. As you read this book, with such community building as a goal, feel free to delve into the mindset of our ten educators. You will find that each teacher writing in this volume represents one you would want for your own child. And you'll become an advocate for other teachers to have similar opportunities for the benefit of more learners.

Sincerely,

Zsa G. Boykin

An Open Letter to College and University Professors Preparing Future Classroom Teachers from Dr. Toby Emert, Assistant Professor of English and English Education

Dear Teacher Educators:

Imagine, if you will, a text designed specifically to elicit critical questions from its readers, not simply to detail conclusions—a book that, in some regards, asks its readers to respond, to add to the stories, to create a dialogue with the book's authors. I grant you that concept hits somewhat outside the boundaries we, in the current educational culture, are accustomed to. We have been taught to expect the stories we read and those we tell to have clear beginnings, clear rising exposition, and clear conclusions. And this expectation about stories spills over into our classrooms where, we are told, we should be paying spectacular attention to conclusions—to the assessment of student performance as it relates to mandated objectives. What we know about the real work that goes on in successful classrooms, however, is that, if nothing else, it is messy, unpredictable, and process-oriented.

This collection of essays by teachers who represent a cross-section of backgrounds, experience, and expertise acknowledges the messiness in our work—in fact, in some ways, they celebrate it. When I was asked to join a group of three other colleagues to respond to this manuscript, I accepted the invitation because I am committed to the idea of helping teachers critique their practices. I was intrigued with the idea of teachers collaborating to form writing groups. In my professional life, which includes work as a theatre director, a classroom teacher, a career counselor, a university administrator, and a professor, I've seen only a few teams who seemed to understand some of the nuances of sharing both responsibilities and rewards. This book gives us the stories of teachers who made a purposeful choice to come together and to share the work of crafting something significant, timely, and useful. In doing so, they came to the project with an eye toward nurturing their own professional growth and an eye toward creating models of collaboration that others may wish to emulate. In short, what the editors of this book have assembled is a diverse set of portraits of teacher-teams working, writing, collaborating, thinking, and, perhaps most importantly, reflecting.

Reflection became a key component in the work that each small group did for the project. Two themes appear frequently in the book: the need for more time to reflect and the need for a structure that supports the reflective analysis of classroom practices. The teacher-writers acknowledge that as they engaged in the process of responding to each other's essays, they began to trust that process. Carol Harrell, another English Education professor, pointed out when I talked with her about her experience participating in the book project, "I didn't trust the idea of offering my writing to others for feedback before this experience. Now, I understand. I'll never look at my classroom in quite the same way again."

The essays in the book stand as evidence that the response group process helped these teacher/writers to internalize the idea of critical reflection. The editors purposefully chose to expose the architecture of the project, inviting other educational professionals to adapt the idea. Using the structure of the process, as outlined in the introduction and in the conclusion, other teacher cohorts in other settings could embark on a similar journey. The book serves as a model for teachers-in-training and for in-service teachers who wish to investigate—with commitment and verve—their own practices through the process of thoughtful collaboration with like-minded colleagues. The book invites us, as we should also invite our students, to re-examine what we think we know about our world and to respond, with passion, to the "messiness" we discover.

Sincerely yours,

Toby Emert, Ph.D.
Assistant Professor of English and English Education

Reflection

And now another confession: we surprised ourselves by how quickly we began to generate workable ideas for a chapter responding to this book. Early in our conversations, we began to make connections to our own teaching practices and philosophies. As our conversations extended, we continued to note our "ah-ha" moments. As for the other authors in this project, we found our collaborative writing opened up more dialogue toward shared professionalization.

We talked about the various settings where we work and how we thought the idea of writing groups could energize teachers who often feel that, despite the deluge of information from a number of agencies and the daily contact with hundreds of students, they plan and deliver instruction in relative isolation. Impromptu conversations in the hallway or the teachers' lounge or the lunchroom do generate new instructional methods or strategies, but generally, teachers have little time for serious reflection on their practices. We were excited about the idea of educators collaborating in an effort to discover how to celebrate the extraordinary moments in their classrooms and how to find ways to encourage more of those moments.

*We thought that idea was revolutionary—that if more teachers engaged in critical conversations about their practices with an eye toward **writing** about what they learned from those conversations, they would come to think of themselves more as professionals—highly trained and extremely thoughtful practitioners who view their work as vital, generative, and specialized. We realize that most teachers are not expected to think of themselves as professionals in the ways physicians, attorneys, and executives do. In contrast, the teachers who participated in the writing groups described in this book expressed major changes in their attitudes about the roles they play in their classrooms. The reflecting and the writing and the discussing validated their efforts and encouraged them to continue to learn and adapt, essentially becoming the "life-long learners" we often say we want our students to become.*

Like the teachers who wrote the other chapters in this book, we found the very process of meeting, writing, talking, and creating a product together encouraged us to expand our individual perspectives. Our group process influenced our individual processes. Our group talk foregrounded our internal dialogues. Our group feedback to the writing each of us was doing encouraged us to revise both the words on the page and the thoughts behind them.

The work we engaged in and the work of the teachers whose articles make up the book mirror the kind of work we want our students to do. These teacher-writers found a wealth of ideas that are influencing who they are in their classrooms and learned, by practice and through feedback, that structured reflection has its strong rewards. This collaboration gave the four of us an opportunity to do that—to begin a dialogue about possibilities—generated from the writing we did.

We discovered that this process opens and enlightens; it touches and personalizes; it instructs and inspires. Isn't that what we want our teaching ultimately to do?

Setting Teachers' Writing Groups in Context

Sarah Robbins, George Seaman, Dede Yow, and Kathleen Blake Yancey

How and why did we use writing groups as both a vehicle for promoting teacher professionalization and a strategy to document and interpret that process? What did we learn from our inquiry? What recommendations would we make to others interested in adapting our process? This chapter takes a retrospective look at ways that our larger community of practice supported our writing groups and, especially, at some of the lessons we learned about meta-level thinking and writing to learn that can help sustain teachers' professionalization projects. We want to make the various components and stages of our project visible to readers so that they can adopt and adapt these practices in their own contexts.

Forming the Community

We began with about a dozen educators who wanted to use shared, structured reflection and writing to examine their teaching critically and, eventually, to share their experiences with a more public audience. George Seaman, an experienced teacher consultant, had suggested we invite teachers at our National Writing Project site to explore links between writing and teacher professionalization. Having sent out a call for volunteers, we assembled initially as an inquiry community of about a dozen teachers. At the start of the project, this inquiry community subdivided into several writing groups, based on a range of factors, including having basic topics of interest in common or living in relative proximity to each other.

Before joining this collaborative initiative, many of us had participated in at least one summer institute sponsored by the Kennesaw Mountain Writing Project (KMWP). While a number of us had published before, or had presented teaching practices to public audiences at conferences, not every one joining the inquiry team had experience writing for professional publication. Before our the first meeting, Sarah Robbins invited Kathleen Blake Yancey to participate, since Kathi's scholarship on writing and reflection was clearly a good fit with our interests.[1] Kathi joined Sarah, George, and Dede Yow as editors. For a project studying communities of practice, shared reflection and writing groups in action, having a team of editors seemed a logical approach. Throughout the collaborative work on this book, in fact, the editors continued to operate as another writing group. We regularly "talked" online about such questions as how to sequence the chapters and how to identify relevant scholarship for ourselves and for all project participants. We exchanged drafts and made comments, adapting protocols from the other writing groups while sharing their core values. In addition, the editorial group served as collaborative facilitators of the entire inquiry community: we often met (in person and online) to plan the sessions held for the whole project team, and we regularly reflected together about the progress of the project.

Inquiry Questions and General Findings

Before our community's first meeting in September 2002, project leaders Robbins, Seaman, Yow, and Yancey drafted several questions linking collaborative reflection, community-building, writing, and professional development.[2] We wondered: what can we learn about our teaching from working in a collaborative community of interlocking writing groups? We also asked: what happens, in terms of reflection as an avenue to growing professionally, when teachers use writing groups as a step toward a more public audience?

We planned from the start to investigate these questions by working in small writing groups within our larger inquiry community, while at the same time studying our processes in action. We formulated the following sub-queries related to our overarching questions:

- How does/can shared reflection in writing groups foster individual and group writing processes?
- Could writing for an audience foster professional growth, and, if so, how? We imagined two stages of "audience" here: the writing group and then some larger public.
- How can collaborative writing and reflection, in writing groups, enhance teachers' view of themselves as professionals? And their view of the teaching profession?
- What might our writing groups and our own community of practice learn from other professional groups' reflective protocols and practices?

As an entire project community, we revisited these questions periodically, often through *structured* reflective writing exercises (e.g., sequenced questions addressed during our large inquiry community meetings). Significantly, all those involved in the project conceived of themselves as investigating these questions both *while and by* working collaboratively on their own piece of writing.[3] Thus, at meetings of individual writing groups and at workshops we held for the entire team, we often moved back and forth between discussing the goals of the project as a whole, and engaging with our own individual pieces of writing. Also, we frequently asked ourselves what our work at a particular small-group or whole-team session "meant" in regard to the project's overarching agenda. Over time, we all became quite accustomed to writing reflectively about what we were learning. Furthermore, from this body of informal writing, we identified ways in which participation in the project promoted a heightened sense of professionalism among our teacher-authors. We also tracked everyone's increased ability to manage the interactions of a writing group and an enhanced understanding of the teaching-related topics being examined through our writing processes. We noted benefits of using *reflection-oriented structures* (such as having everyone respond to the same sequenced, written queries), and we learned to use our writing groups themselves as a *semi-private/semi-public way station* preparing teachers to reach larger audiences.

Chronology of Our Work

Deep learning, applicable to a range of diverse contexts, takes time to build, as we learned in our project. While various groups' *initial* work on their essays was sometimes concentrated in less than a year's time, our shared study of the *social practices* undergirding that process—and its implications for other teachers—took much longer.

Our collaborative inquiry formally began with a day-long workshop for all potential participants in September of 2002. Through the 2002-03 academic year, and again during the summer, participants met several times in the small writing groups that we formed during that first September workshop. Meanwhile, we held our second day-long workshop for the entire inquiry community in March of 2003 and a third workshop for initial revision and reflection during the summer of 2003. During the fall of 2003, the editors began to organize the essays and reflections into a draft book manuscript. In the winter of 2004, a four-person team of "first readers" wrote individual reactions to the manuscript and then collaborated on a group response. In the spring and summer of 2004, the four editors drafted the opening and closing chapters of the book. During the 2004-05 academic year, and the summer of 2005, we did additional revisions of essays in response to suggestions from more readers (e.g., attendees at the summer institutes of our National Writing Project site). By spring 2005, participants had enough distance from our original work together to be able to reflect with insight into how the various writing groups had functioned, on what their impact was on our individual essays, and on what we had learned from the project as a whole. So, in June 2005, all project members responded in writing to structured questions about the writing groups in action and about the significance of the larger community's activities for their learning. We then crafted group-voiced introductions to each cluster of essays and revised (in this case, extended) the reflections we had outlined earlier about the social composing processes that produced our essays. We also collaborated on extensive revisions of the introductory and closing chapters of the book. All along the way, we tried to step outside of our writing processes to analyze how they were working—both to promote our text-making itself and to learn more about our own teaching.

Project Design: Core Values for Writing and Professionalization

We envisioned the basic structure of our project as a collection of circles, with our three small writing groups clustered together as a community of practice seeking to forge connections with scholarship on social literacy practices, on professional development grounded in shared reflection, and on writing as an avenue to learning. From the start, we planned that the small writing groups would be meeting in between those occasions when the large group assembled. At the same time, building on the example of Janet Swenson and her colleagues in the Write for Your Life Project, we promoted ongoing communication between the small writing groups and the larger inquiry community with a project listserv, where the four editors and all other participants could post reminders, queries, and comments. The listserv was sometimes inactive for weeks at a time, but would burst back into life when prompted by a member's request for information or a report on responses from readers of our manuscript.

Clearly, one core value everyone had in common—as underscored by participants' reliable responses to any online queries and their enthusiastic participation in the small groups—was the desire to develop a "sense of belonging to a larger community that comes from writing" (Durst 262). Indeed, *belonging together* as writers helped us generate and, gradually, extend our texts and our thinking. The attraction of writing to create and sustain community remained powerful. In that regard, when we wrote reflections about the project in the summer of 2005, many participants described "missing" the regular meetings of their small writing groups and also called on the project leaders to organize a reunion of the entire inquiry community.

Though participants certainly appreciated membership in our immediate community, they also conceived of those ties as opening up avenues to additional professional forms of belonging, as represented by the professional reading we did together in small groups and on the larger team. But, from the outset, writing was the most crucial component of our learning, moving us from the typical privacy of classroom teaching to expanded social interaction and knowing. Both the writing done in the inquiry community (e.g., on the listserv, at in-person gatherings) and the text-making orchestrated by the small writing groups acted, all along, in a kind of "in-between" space for reflection and writing *toward* a more public discourse. On the one hand, for example, writing in our small groups—whether on a napkin during a restaurant meeting or in the margins of a colleague's draft—allowed us to try out ideas and share tentative observations in a supportive, safe environment. On the other hand, and often at the same time, shared reflective writing for the project moved our thinking beyond such private realms as personal journals (see Hays and Holly) to a semi-public space. Pushed to write with and for others, we had to give our tentative thoughts some form, and responses from others further refined tentative texts.

Whether at our whole community meetings, on the listserv, or in writing group sessions, we consistently affirmed the value of writing to learn as supporting our efforts to form community. Much of the writing *around* our essay-composing took on exploratory modes—tentative and formative rather than finished. The practice of sharing such writing to move thinking forward affiliated our work with concepts laid out by James Britton, Toby Fulwiler, and Art Young, who have emphasized that expressive (versus more finished, persuasive writing) "is not [produced] to communicate, but to order and represent experience to our own understanding," thereby offering "a tool for discovering, for shaping meaning, and for reaching understanding."[4] In line with Peter Elbow's arguments favoring "Writing for Learning," we viewed our frequent reflective writing occasions as "low stakes writing," aiming "to learn, understand, remember and figure out what [we didn't] yet know," rather than to report on what we already understood. In particular, consistent with Art Young's formulation of a "middle ground" between writing to learn and writing to communicate, we tried to structure the social composing space of our writing groups and our larger inquiry community as a transitional discourse between the personal and the public, between the private reflections a teacher might jot down in a notebook and the finished teacher research articles we all admire but can't always un-pack as having been in-process at some point. To help ourselves move from reflections drafted on our own to a "finished" piece of writing about our teaching, but to leave behind traces of the process that other teachers could later follow, we aimed to enact the kind of conversational composing Young has associated with "middleground" writing. We saw our reflective pieces, especially, as bridging writing-to-learn texts and writing-to-communicate products—as semipublic, collaborative writing that would be "enabling" for us.[5] At the same time, through our efforts to create and save *artifacts of social reflection*, and then to reflect *about* them again later, we hoped to make our processes available as models for other teachers interested in our work and in their own writing goals. In taking this approach, we were trying to integrate promising practices from the writing-to-learn movement with research on reflective practitioners.[6]

Small Writing Groups at Work

Our inquiry community's core values for writing to learn led us to promote specific social composing strategies for the small writing groups by trying them out during the whole-team sessions. For example, we used and thus affirmed approaches such as combining oral with written response; offering positive comments before making suggestions for improvement; and critiquing our own techniques for shared reflection by asking: "Why are we doing this practice the way we are doing it?" In addition, as a whole inquiry community, we discussed scholarship on our research questions; we set deadlines that would apply to the whole group; and we had small groups share reports of their progress on the listserv and at our day-long workshops. Taken together, these *orchestrated practices* shaped the larger community itself, while modeling adaptable approaches for the small writing groups to sample, critique, and refine.

Nonetheless, as indicated by the prefatory piece for each section of our book, despite the shared belief system our large-community connections nurtured, every small writing group did develop its own distinctive strategies of operation, ranging from different schedules for meetings to different activities in those sessions, and each developed its own protocols. (See introduction.) In some cases, these variations grew out of differing needs participants brought to their groups. For instance, one group began the project with drafts on hand while another had two members with nothing but a topic in mind. In other cases, the variations in approaches for collaboration developed through careful discussion of what was working well for the group and what needed to be changed.[7]

Our writing groups also varied in the degree to which members would describe them as successful at different stages in the overall life of the project, and in the features of the work they would invoke to characterize their progress. In one group, for instance, the task of drafting and revising members' essays, in and of itself, took precedence, and they measured success largely by marking deadlines met while making substantial revisions. In another group, unstructured, shared reflection about professional experiences actually became at least as important as composing the essays. In the third group, writing the essays and building social relationships were self-consciously designated as complementary aims all along—and that group's protocols for working were clearly consistent with such a view. Despite these differences, all members of all groups identified a number of important benefits they associated with having participated in the project; furthermore, the benefits they named were consistent across groups: becoming better writers, becoming more reflective about teaching, reaching an audience beyond the classroom, acquiring self-confidence, growing as a professional, and building personal relationships grounded in shared professionalism.

The fact that all participants in the inquiry project came to compatible conclusions about the benefits of the work was consistent, we later found, with our having assumed important characteristics for organized social learning as identified by Richard McDermott in "Knowing Community: 10 Critical Factors in Building Communities of Practice." (Significantly, rather than using McDermott's traits as a kind of "recipe," we instead gradually took on the traits he describes on our own, then discovered his profile during the final stages of writing this book, as we were seeking to understand our work in a broader context of related research.) According to McDermott, communities of practice assemble and use tacit knowledge, share strongly held interests and values, and thrive on trust supported by personal interaction. McDermott identifies a number of factors that he dubs "critical to the success of communities of practice," including focusing on topics important to members, providing time and encouragement for participation, drawing on core values held in common, fostering personal relationships, creating formal opportunities "for thinking together as well as systems for sharing information," ensuring shared access to the community's knowledge base and knowledge-making practices, and facilitating genuine dialogue about issues of importance to community members. In retrospect, we can see how the interactions between our small writing groups and the larger inquiry team we assembled for this project enabled us to tap into the success factors McDermott identifies. Thus, a key reason for sharing our work is to enable other groups of teachers to adapt our practices for sponsoring writing groups to their own local context in ways that will build communities of practice to support educators' professionalization.

For readers who want to draw on our project as a model for supporting teacher professionalization, the experience of one "failed" writing group is also important to note. Though the three writing groups whose essays appear in our book continued working together through all phases of the project, a fourth disengaged early on. This group, originally comprised of Terri Holbrook, Mary

Lynn Huie, and Kathi Yancey, disbanded without ever having a formal meeting that included all three members. Kathi Yancey did remain connected to the project as a member of the editorial writing group, but Teri and Mary Lynn, though active affiliates of our National Writing Project site, both withdrew. In an evaluation written during the winter of 2003, they observed:

> Both of us have been in writing groups before, so thinking about how and why this one did not work has been instructional.... If we had met more often, we might have recognized our group problems and contacted one of the members of the larger group for help.... We were supposed to have been a community within a larger community with a shared purpose. But somehow, we were too isolated from the larger group both physically and mentally to make contact for support when we should have.

Whole-Community Meetings and Progressive Stages in the Work

As Mary Lynn's and Teri's assessment suggests, small writing groups may be less likely to succeed if their members fail to establish and maintain connections with larger social structures potentially supporting their work. For this project, although the small writing groups may well have been most responsible for shaping our authors' individual essays, the whole-community gatherings also played a vital role in that process, as well as in our investigation of overarching questions. Along those lines, whereas much of the work situated within our small writing groups maintained a focus on classroom practices and on specific techniques for preparing professional writing, the analysis we did in our larger community extended our inquiry to the type Glenda L. Bissex has described as "more interpretive than pragmatic," beyond "collecting practical strategies" for teaching to "gaining understandings and awareness" (92).

In activities for the larger inquiry community, to promote reflective analysis, we emphasized that all our small writing groups were investigating the same global inquiry questions even as they were nurturing the individual composing efforts of each teacher-author. In general, our larger community of practice was focused on setting our small groups' evolving activities in a broader context of research, on drawing comparative inferences from our groups' reports of their work, and on feeding those observations back into our small-group practices interactively (so that we were constantly "testing out" hypotheses through the actual practices/protocols of our writing groups). Accordingly, we used the occasions when the whole inquiry team assembled to interpret the progress of the small writing groups. With jigsaw activities and whole-team discussions, we would set individual groups in dialogue with each other. We then considered the implications of our experiences for research in such areas as writing to learn and teachers' reflective professionalization. All of us recognized—and even joked about—the "meta" level of work that these whole-community meetings entailed. In retrospect, we can identify several important stages in our learning. These stages of professionalization through our project may well be helpful to others adapting our model.

Phase One: Social Brainstorming—
Raising Questions and Providing Working Time

As Kathleen Yancey emphasized at our September 2002 kick-off session, crucial to our investigation was an acknowledgement that the teaching profession rarely gives organized time or systems to reflection-based learning. To illustrate that point, Kathi shared research she had been doing on physicians' communities of practice. She challenged us to see what we might learn from their emphasis on collaborative reflection to analyze both specific incidents in the classroom and promising practices for teaching.

Through discussion, we identified ways that physicians' collaborative examination of their practices could serve as something of a model—particularly in their emphasis on regularity, systematic critique, and reflection. But we also realized that our own shared reflection for professional growth would make more explicit and sustained use of *writing* to learn than the medical profession's oral critiques of its practices do. So we aimed to become a discussion-oriented community of practice. But we also established from the outset that we would ask *how and to what effect the writing done through our small groups would shape our professionalization*. Toward that end, early in our first session, we asked everyone to draft a scene from teaching, then to read and discuss that scene with a colleague, then to consider what role the writing and discussion had played in clarifying the experience behind the scene. At the close of our first day-long workshop, we all wrote about our individual responses to these terms: reflection, writing, and teaching. And we considered how those terms might be interactively related through the protocols that we would establish in our writing groups.

One pattern that emerged in this first set of focused freewrites was participants' recognition of the powerful learning promoted just by having an *occasion* to reflect and using *writing* as a vehicle for thinking. One community member's comments seemed typical: "I teach all the time, and I write all the time, but I never have time to reflect. Today, I had protected time to reflect.

The writing we did helped my reflecting. I know that both these things will feed into my teaching." Another project goal emerged from whole-community discussion on our kick-off day: establishing regular systems for working in our writing groups—"rules" we could count on like the physicians whose regularized discussions Kathi had described. Looking back, we can certainly point to ways our writing groups benefited from this session, which identified core values for the whole inquiry community, established overarching inquiry questions, and provided some examples of promising practices for collaborative learning. Therefore, we would recommend that others seeking to facilitate teachers' writing groups for professional growth begin with an occasion of shared goal-setting. That strategy helps participants position their work in larger professional contexts, identify possible working practices, and feel empowered to take on challenging topics in a supportive environment.

Phase Two: Generating Texts—
Reflecting on Process and Sharing Working Strategies

The second whole-community meeting was held in March 2003. On that occasion, we spent a good deal of time hearing from each writing group about the protocols they had developed, and why those approaches were the ones they had adopted. For instance, one group described the role that "digital blue-penciling" was playing when they exchanged drafts via email attachments. Sharing such specific strategies gave each group new ideas. Perhaps more importantly, however, we spent some time writing and then thinking together, more globally, about how the work of the small writing groups was connecting reflection to enhanced understanding of teaching.[8] Observations included the point that one group made about writing "forcing you to examine your teaching philosophy in order to put your thoughts on paper." That same group also observed that their collaborative work on their essays had generated a "shared ownership of teaching stories" that in turn led to a heightened sense of teaching as public work. In a collaborative composing and revision space, which that group had begun to term "the semi-private stage" of writing, these teachers were finding that their group activity was indeed promoting learning about teaching, and they could identify specific lessons they had learned. Much of what they had done in their small-group meetings, they suggested, could "not have happened in the big group," because the intimacy of their meetings actually enabled more intense, sustained conversations.

Hearing such observations from the small groups, in turn, led all of us to note that the writing groups we had been using had both *structure and intimacy*. We built on these observations to create personal reflections describing ways that "belonging to" and "participating in" both our large inquiry community and our small writing groups were helping us reflect critically on our teaching, on our writing, and on the very process of learning through social reflection. Significantly, one theme that emerged from these focused freewrites, when the editors later read them as a set, was an enhanced sense of professional identity.[9] We could see that participants were moving from a view of their teaching as primarily personal to a sense of their work as publicly significant and therefore worthy of public representation and analysis. We could also see how self-conscious affiliation with both their small writing group and the larger inquiry community was supporting that growth. Based on the generative discussions we had that day, we realized that our project had moved into a new stage, one enabling us to reflect on process and describe it to others, then use those exchanges to further refine our working practices. Therefore, we suggest others who facilitate teachers' writing groups should create occasions when those groups can share protocols, write and think about their practices, and then identify ways such sharing can feed back into the work of the groups interactively—all the while heightening professional self-awareness.

Phase Three: Revising and Re-vising— Reaching Across Writing Groups and into Professionalization

In June of 2003, we held what we called a "mini-institute" at Kennesaw State. We hoped to analyze these components of our work: small-group protocols for collaborative reflection and writing; interactions between our three writing groups and the larger inquiry community; and the impact that participation in the project was having on all of us professionally. We had been considering these questions all along, but this occasion served as a major "checkpoint" in the process. Our work for this all-day session focused on the processes that had shaped our individual essays rather than on the essays themselves. All participants were asked, before this June gathering, to read an essay from a group other than their own. To prepare for this workshop, we all drafted the following pieces of writing:

- A written response to an essay authored by someone outside our original writing group (These cross-group assignments were made by the editorial team, based on topic connections across the essays.);
- A set of "starter draft" notes about the ways in which our essay had been influenced by our participation in our small writing group (These notes would eventually become the reflective pieces appended to the end of each contributor's individual essays.);

- Ideas for a piece we would eventually write collaboratively with our writing group members to describe the protocols we had developed.

Besides working on the three pieces identified above, we also spent time during the day-long session writing about and discussing our "big-picture" inquiry questions. In on-the-spot writing, we described how the project had changed us professionally. Here are a few examples:

Leslie Walker: My professional identity has emerged stronger than it has ever been.... Although I have always had the commitment to teaching, working with others who have the same commitment strengthens my resolve. Sometimes one can get lost in one's own classroom. It helps to be associated with a professional enterprise...to bring me out of my high school classroom and to enjoy the intellectual discourse of a community of learners. The practice of reflecting—especially through writing—is an exercise that facilitates and sustains professional growth.

Debby Kramb: I came into this project with a strong commitment to teaching. But I had reached a point in my career when I was reaching out—striving for "something more".... My personal identity as a teacher and a capable, intelligent person has been strengthened.... My confidence and self-esteem as a professional continue to grow.

Renee Kaplan: I feel more energized and empowered as a community of professional writers and learners who are committed to student achievement.... Collaboration and sharing...have become the energetic fuel that we all used, shared, and are storing now for future use.

Our whole-group discussion of these freewrites represented one of the most powerful learning occasions of our inquiry project. Sharing our individual notes with each other, we could identify recurring patterns—literally new ideas about our own professional identities—that had emerged from belonging to our project. We could also feel shared excitement and pride in our achievements. Though we realized our essays still required extensive revision, we knew we had all written something significant about our teaching. In addition, examining our practices through writing and reading drafts from other groups built a sense that we were starting to become members of a larger "scholarly community," beyond our own writing groups. Reflecting and writing together, we had all found new professional voices, stronger professional identities.

Our project participants wound up extending the reflective writing we sponsored at this stage in a number of productive ways. Some made significant revisions in their essays based on reading a piece from another writing group. Some started drawing on the language we were using in the whole-community reflections to help manage other learning situations in which they were engaged, such as graduate programs or professional committees. Given such results, we recommend that others who facilitate networks of teachers' writing groups should create multiple opportunities for participants to share their learning, write reflectively about how they are learning, and situate their work in broader contexts.

Phase Four: Publishing—Connecting with Multiple Audiences, Reshaping Learning in New Contexts

During the 2004-05 school year, George attended a district-wide inservice program where Andy Smith, one of our participants, spoke energetically about his involvement with this project and described his excitement about editing his essay with eventual publication in mind. After that presentation, George asked the other members of the editing team: *Did setting a book-publishing goal relatively early in our process (i.e., in winter of 2003) mean that the work seemed more crucial? Did having that goal give our work greater meaning than a 'typical' cluster of teachers' writing groups—one not aiming for book publication—might attain?*

We suspect the answer to George's first "setting the goal" question is "yes." Although we did not start out with a definite timetable for manuscript preparation, and although we consistently used the term "hope" when discussing our book-publishing aims, at a certain point, when the texts started to grow and we began to read across writing groups, having a published product did begin to seem achievable. Then, the pace of work certainly picked up. In addition, as happens with all types of "publication" endeavors (including posting kids' writing in a school hallway), project participants began to pay more attention to details of style, editing, and citation formatting. Writing that is aimed at a formal public audience easily claims careful attention.

However, we can now firmly answer "no" to George's second question. At a certain point in our project, we realized participants were already publishing our work in a wide variety of venues: whether or not we ever successively disseminated our story in printed book, we had successfully reached a "publishing" stage that was important to professional growth. Like Andy at the district inservice conference, many members of our inquiry community were beginning to share material from our essays with colleagues, and to share stories about the processes and implications of our writing groups and the larger inquiry community that supported them. In school-level inservice, professional development programs organized by our local National Writing

Project site, and conferences sponsored by other professional organizations, our project team members were reporting on our work in ways that enhanced their own professionalization.

We were also feeding our writing for the project—and our learning from it—into a whole array of new writing products and professional roles. Vicki Walker used strategies from her writing group's meetings and reflective writing about their protocols to guide her design of curriculum for several inservice courses she facilitated for elementary, middle, and high school teachers. Carol Harrell used her writing for this project—and her learning about writing groups—to help lead a professional team of university professors writing about a standards program. George Seaman drew on his writing in our inquiry community—both in his writing group and in the editorial team—to support the reflective assessment processes of National Board certification. Leslie Walker confidently joined a team of Atlanta-area educators collaborating to write curriculum aimed at improving local race relations. Debby Kramb used her enhanced writing abilities, along with her increased self-confidence as a leader, to become a mentor for students in a graduate program, thereby expanding her professional role from elementary school classroom teacher to teacher educator. Renee Kaplan wrote about her participation in this project when applying for a prestigious national educational award—which she subsequently won.

Whatever the publications that continue to grow out of this project, heightened perceptions about ourselves as professionals may be the most important "product" of teachers' writing groups. How teachers perceive themselves certainly affects the professional choices and social contributions that they make—in the classroom and beyond. Through participation in our inquiry community, teachers used shared reflection and social writing to shore up their professional identities. Viewing our colleagues' stories and writing as a powerful source of learning, as well as hearing others respond to our own writing in the same respectful way, all of us came to see our teaching differently, to speak with greater confidence. We used the social process of writing together to learn and grow professionally. We now invite readers to adapt our model for what we expect would be equally powerful results.

Endnotes

[1] See "The Teaching Circle" and *Reflection in the Writing Classroom*.

[2] See Hubbard and Power on inquiry questions in action research.

[3] See McLaughlin, Shanahan, and Wortham.

[4] See "An Introduction to WAC."

[5] See Young's *Teaching Writing Across the Curriculum*, 57 and 56

[6] Schön, "Concluding Remarks"; Schön, *The Reflective Turn*; Norlander-Case, Reagan and Case, *The Professional Teacher*.

[7] See, in that vein, advice from Birchak and colleagues in *Teacher Study Groups*, including ideas for dealing with conflict in groups, 118-120.

[8] See McDonald, Morh, Dichter, and McDonald, especially Chapter 4.

[9] See Wortham's discussion of "a dialogic approach" to social learning, leading to "understanding and self as emerging within multivoiced conversations" positioned within ongoing "verbal practices"—160-61.

References

"An Introduction to WAC: A Fuller Definition of Writing to Learn." 2006. WAC Clearinghouse. 10 July 2005 <http://wac.colostate.edu/intro/pop4a.cfm>.

Birchak, Barb, Clay Connor, Kathleen Marie Crawford, Leslie Kahn, Sandy Kaser, Susan Turner, and Kathy G. Short. *Teacher Study Groups: Building Community through Dialogue and Reflection*. Urbana: NCTE, 1998.

Bissex, Glenda L. "Teacher Research: Seeing What We Are Doing." *Teachers Thinking, Teachers Knowing: Reflections on Literacy and Language Education*. Ed. Timothy Shanahan. Urbana: NCTE, 1994. 88-104.

Durst, Russel K. "A Writer's Community: How Teachers Can Form Writing Groups." *Teacher as Writer: Entering the Professional Conversation*. Ed. K. L. Dahl. Urbana: NCTE, 1992. 261-72.

Elbow, Peter. "Writing for Learning—Not Just for Demonstrating Learning." *The National Teaching and Learning Forum*. 2004. 10 July 2005 <http://www.ntlf.com/html/lib/bib/writing.htm>.

Holly, Mary Louise. *Writing to Grow: Keeping a Personal-Professional Journal*. Portsmouth: Heinemann, 1989.

Hubbard, Ruth Shagoury, and Brenda Miller Power. *The Art of Classroom Inquiry: A Handbook for Teacher Researchers*. Portsmouth: Heinemann, 1993.

McDermott, Richard. "Knowing in Community: 10 Critical Success Factors in Building Communities of Practice." 2000. Community Intelligence Labs. 27 Sept. 2006 <http://www.co-i-l.com/coil/knowledge-garden/cop/knowing.shtml>.

McDonald, Joseph P., Nancy Mohr, Alan Dichter, and Elizabeth C. McDonald. *The Power of Protocols: An Educator's Guide to Better Practice*. New York: Teachers College Press, 2003.

McLaughlin, Milbrey Wallin. "Strategic Sites for Teachers' Professional Development." *Teacher Development and the Struggle for Authenticity: Professional Growth and Restructuring in the Context of Change*. Ed. Peter P. Grimmett and Jonathan Neufeld. New York: Teachers College Press, 1994. 31-51.

Norlander-Case, Kay A., Timothy G. Reagan, and Charles W. Case. *The Professional Teacher: The Preparation and Nurturance of the Reflective Practitioner*. San Francisco: Jossey-Bass, 1999.

Schön, Donald A. "Concluding Remarks." *The Reflective Turn: Case Studies in and on Educational Practice*. Ed. Donald A. Schön. New York: Teachers College Press, 1991. 343-59.

---, ed. *The Reflective Turn: Case Studies in and on Educational Practice*. New York: Teachers College Press, 1991.

Senge, Peter M., Nelda Cambron-McCabe, Timothy Lucas, Bryan Smith, Janis Dutton, and Art Kleiner. *Schools that Learn: A Fifth Discipline Fieldbook for Educators, Parents, and Everyone Who Cares About Education.* New York: Currency/Doubleday, 2000.

Shanahan, Timothy, ed. *Teachers Thinking, Teachers Knowing: Reflections on Literacy and Language Education.* Urbana: NCTE, 1994.

Swenson, Janet. "Transformative Teacher Networks, On-Line Professional Development, and the Write for Your Life Project." *English Education* 35 (2003): 262-320.

Wortham, Stanton. *Narratives in Action: A Strategy for Research and Analysis.* New York: Teachers College Press, 2001.

Yancey, Kathleen Blake. *Reflection in the Writing Classroom.* Logan: Utah State UP, 1998.

---. "The Teaching Circle, the WPA, and the Work of Writing in the University." *Kitchen Cooks, Plate Twirlers, and Troubadours: Writing Administrators Tell Their Stories.* Ed. Diana George. Portsmouth: Heinemann, 1999. 129-138.

Young, Art. *Teaching Writing Across the Curriculum.* 3rd ed. Upper Saddle River: Prentice Hall, 1999.

Author Profiles

Zsa Boykin holds a B.B.A. and B.S.E. from Georgia State University and a Masters of Education from Kennesaw State University. She presently teaches sixth, seventh, and eighth grade gifted students at Lindley Middle School, a Leonard Bernstein/Grammy Foundation Artful Learning School, in Mableton, Georgia. Zsa was a 1996 Fellow of the Kennesaw Mountain Writing Project (KMWP) and since then has served the National Writing Project site as a member of the Project Outreach Leadership Team, Summer Institute Mentor, and Chair of the Advisory Council. Zsa was her school's 2003-2004 Teacher of the Year.

Toby Emert is an assistant professor in the Education Department at Agnes Scott College. He specializes in courses for future language arts teachers, and he draws on his background in theater, counseling, and diversity education to create learning spaces that are both imaginative and nurturing for his students. Earlier in his career, he taught English and drama in middle and high school and coached competitive forensics teams. His creative and scholarly writing appears, among other places, in *The ALAN Review; Borderlands, The Texas Poetry Review; The Oregon Review; Zone 3; The Panhandler;* and *Combating Heterosexism: Strategies that Work* (Columbia University Press).

Sandra Grant has taught middle and high school English to gifted, honors, and ESOL students in Florida and Georgia. Before becoming a teacher, she worked in the business sector and holds a masters degree in management and human resources. Sandra received her Educational Leadership Certification in June 2003 from Kennesaw State University. She served as Chair of the KMWP Advisory Council, 2002-2003. Sandra is currently an English teacher and the Writing Coordinator at South Cobb High School.

Carol P. Harrell teaches in the English Education program at Kennesaw State University but taught middle and high school English for fifteen years. She has worked with writing projects in Florida and Indiana, and she leads teachers workshops in Atlanta on the teaching of writing and reading. During the last few years Carol directed, as part of a federal School-to-Work Grant, the Kennesaw Regional Business and Education Collaborative, a partnership between business and education leaders, a project designed to ease students' transition from the school setting to the work environment. She currently directs a federal GEAR UP partnership grant.

Renee Kaplan, a KMWP teacher consultant, received her B.A. from the University of South Florida and M.Ed. from the University of Miami. A National Board Certified teacher, she instructs eighth grade language arts at Mabry Middle School, Cobb County, Georgia. She also serves as a Regional Museum Educator of the United States Holocaust Memorial Museum and designs national educational programs. She received the 2004 Spirit of Anne Frank Educator Award from the Anne Frank Center in New York and the 2005 Distinguished Educator Award from the Georgia Commission on the Holocaust. She has been a recipient of numerous teacher fellowships.

Deborah Kramb, a Nationally Certified teacher, is a K-5 math facilitator for Cobb County School District north of Atlanta, where she served as a mentor teacher to student and first-year teachers. She has taught fifth grade and a multi-age class in a Title One school as well as bilingual kindergarten and first grade in Orange County, California. She has her Master's Degree in Reading from California State University, Fullerton, and her Education Specialist Degree in Early Childhood Education from Georgia State University, where she is currently working on a Ph.D. She serves as a teacher consultant through the Kennesaw Mountain Writing Project and has presented on Differentiation and Writing at the Primary Level for university audiences.

Sarah Robbins is author of *Managing Literacy, Mothering America: Women's Narratives on Reading and Writing in the Nineteenth Century* (University of Pittsburgh Press) and of *The Cambridge Introduction to Harriet Beecher Stowe* (Cambridge University Press). She is co-editor of *Writing America: Classroom Literacy and Public Engagement* (Teachers College Press) and *Writing Our Communities: Local Learning and Public Culture* (NCTE). A K-12 teacher for over fifteen years, she is director of Kennesaw State's National Writing Project site. She has also co-directed numerous public scholarship programs in the humanities, including Domesticating the Secondary Canon, Making American Literatures, and Keeping and Creating American Communities.

George Seaman has worked in the Cobb County School District for sixteen years. During that time he has taught British Literature and World Literature. He has also taught freshman composition at Kennesaw State University. He attended the summer institute of the Kennesaw Mountain Writing Project in 1996 and later served as Chair of the Advisory Council. In 2002 he earned National Board Certification and has worked twice as an assessor for the National Board.

Andrew Smith is Supervisor of Professional Development for Cobb County Schools. Andrew has been involved in the Kennesaw Mountain Writing Project since the summer of 1996, including working with the High School Honors Program and serving as a Summer Institute Teacher Mentor and Continuity Program Co-Director. He earned both undergraduate and graduate degrees from Kennesaw State University's English Department.

W. Scott Smoot teaches drama and history to grades 6-8 at The Walker School, an independent school north of Atlanta. He received his Master of Arts in Professional Writing at Kennesaw State University in 2001. For the Keeping and Creating American Communities project, he led students to create an original musical from real-life family stories. His essay on that process was published in *Writing America* (Teacher's College Press, 2004). With the Kennesaw Mountain Writing Project, he has served as creative-writer-in-residence and as a teacher consultant developing smarter ways to use technology in the classroom. His writings and musical compositions can be sampled at www.smootpage.com.

Linda Stewart is an English instructor at Kennesaw State University. At the University of New Hampshire, she earned a Master of Arts in Teaching and a Master of Arts in English Literature. She served as pilot teacher coordinator for the "Keeping and Creating American Communities" project and as faculty co-director for the KMWP site. Conference presentations include CCCC, WPA, GCTE, NCTE, ASA, the Virginia Woolf Conference, the Oklahoma State NWP, and the Georgia-Carolina Conference. She also contributed essays to *Writing America: Classroom Literacy and Public Engagement* and *Writing Our Communities: Local Learning and Public Culture*.

Leslie Walker teaches AP and tenth-grade Literature/Composition at Campbell High School. She earned both her B.S. in Secondary English Education and her Master of Arts in Professional Writing at Kennesaw State University. Leslie was a 1998 Summer Institute fellow of the KMWP and led one of the curriculum teams for the Keeping and Creating American Communities program. Her teacher research essays have been published in *Writing America* (Teachers College Press) and *Writing Our Communities* (NCTE).

Victoria Walker holds a B.S. in Early Childhood Education and a Master of Arts in Professional Writing from Kennesaw State. She has taught students from kindergarten to fifth grade and is currently working with kindergarten students at Mountain Road Elementary. Vicki has been affiliated with the Kennesaw Mountain Writing project since 1997. At the KMWP summer institute, she has held leadership roles as a reading/writing group coach and a creative-writer-in-residence, and she has also served as Chair of the Advisory Council.

Kathleen Blake Yancey is the Kellogg W. Hunt Professor of English at Florida State University, where she directs the graduate program in rhetoric and composition. An upcoming president of NCTE, she is past Chair of the NCTE College Section, past President of the Council of Writing Program Administrators, and the past Chair of the Conference on Composition and Communication. She has co-edited, edited, or authored several books, among them the recent *Teaching Literature as Reflective Practice* (NCTE). A former co-director of the National Writing Project site at the University of North Carolina in Charlotte, she has written over forty articles and book chapters and consults widely on issues and topics connected to K-12 composition and writing across the curriculum.

Dede Yow is on the English faculty at Kennesaw State University. She teaches courses in Southern Literature and gender studies, and she has published essays on Southern fiction writers Mary Hood, Larry Brown, and Bobbie Ann Mason. She co-directed Kennesaw State's 1995 NEH Summer Institute "Domesticating the Secondary Canon," developing a curriculum program for middle and secondary teachers of English and history. She is currently serving as a Faculty Fellow for Diversity Across the Curriculum in KSU's Center for Excellence in Teaching and Learning, and she is co-authoring a history of Kennesaw State University with Professor Tom Scott of the History Department.

Printed in the United States
116930LV00001B/72/A